To Rev John Dr...
with fond memories of our...
I hope you will enjoy reading my book!

Kerry William
III

Led by the Spirit of Truth

My Life Story

Gerald Ivar Williams

This book is dedicated to the
nine most influential women in my life.

My two courageous grandmothers who left Sweden
as teenagers and sailed alone to America:
Mathilda (Johnson) Strom and Hulda (Larson) Williams.

My two loving mothers, Elmie Mildred Strom, who brought me
into this world at risk to her own life and bequeathed to me and
my siblings her strong faith in our Savior Jesus, and Viola Elizabeth
Grisim, who committed to raising me into a proper gentleman.

My two devoted wives, Lorraine Laura (Hoffman) Williams,
who smoothed my rough edges, supported my dreams, and made
me into the God-fearing man that I am now, and Florraine Flora
(Hoffman Wangen Trygstad) Williams who filled the void in my
life after Lorraine left to be with our Lord and until she too left
to be with our Lord and her twin sister Lorraine.

My three overachieving daughters:
Elizabeth Ann Williams Gomoll, Susan Carol (Williams) Jenkins, M.D.
and Jody Renee (Wangen) Hoffman.

Led by the Spirit of Truth

Fram! Fram! St. Olaf
The St. Olaf College Hymn

This hymn is very meaningful to me. I memorized it as a first-year student at St. Olaf College in 1946. As I look back over my life, I came to realize the strength and direction in my life came from the Spirit of God. I chose one line from that hymn for the title of my life story. (Words by Dr. Oscar Overby, music by Dr. F. Melius Christiansen.)

Christmen, Crossmen in dauntless quest,
Led by the spirit of truth,
Running the race, pursuing our quest,
Filled with the song of youth.
Founded in faith to render light,
Radiant today it crowns the height,
Rising glorious and, under God, victorious.

Chorus
Fram! Fram! St. Olaf! Impelled we sing,
Sing to thee.
Fram! Fram! St. Olaf!
The hilltops ring,
Fram! Fram! Free!

Grant that spirit to lead us still
Onward as ages unroll,
Caught by the Crossmen shrined on the hill,
Steepled to lift the soul,
Give us again the heart aglow
Stirred by the songs of Manitou,
Ever glorious and, under God, victorious.

Repeat Chorus

Table of Contents

FOREWARD

I became interested in genealogy late in life as I prepared to retire from my work with Williams Sound Corp. I reflected on what I had accomplished during my sixty years. I also thought about how blessed I had been and how much that I owed to my Swedish immigrant grandparents who made it possible for me to have such a rich and productive life.

My grandfather, Alvin Williams, came to America as a one-year old with his parents and three siblings. They arrived on a sailing vessel at Quebec, Canada, in 1869. My other three grandparents came individually as teenagers aboard steamships in the 1880's.

When I began collecting information about them I realized how little was readily available. Grandpa Alvin Williams died in 1936 when I was only nine years old. Grandma Hulda Williams died in 1945 while I was away serving in the U.S. Navy during World War II. Grandpa John Strom died in 1952 and Grandma Mathilda Strom in 1965, so they were gone before my interest in genealogy had kindled.

Each of them led very interesting lives, but they were Swedes and unassuming people. They would deny they were special in any way. Sadly, they were no longer living when I longed to know all about their lives. What I would give for just a few hours with each of them now!

Instead, I have had to glean bits of their stories from my limited childhood memories and from those who had known them. I thought I would get some help from my parents and their siblings, yet when I asked the answer was usually, "Well, we never talked about that."

So, to my grandchildren and great-grandchildren I have written my life story for you to read when you are old enough to wonder about Papa Jerry and Grandma Lorraine and what they did with God's gift of time on this earth to try to make it a better world.

Gerald "Papa Jerry" Ivar Williams
Northfield, Minnesota
2020

Chapter 1

MY EARLY LIFE

My father, Marland Reinhold Williams, M.D., was the second of four children born to Alvin and Hulda (Larson) Williams, immigrants from Gränna and Hova, Sweden, respectively. My mother, Elmie Mildred Strom, was the third child born to John and Mathilda (Johnson) Strom who were also Swedish immigrants. Marland and Elmie were married on August 11, 1923, in St. Paul, Minnesota.

In the summer of 1927, First Lutheran Church in St. Paul offered jobs to my father and mother to be the director and cook for Bay Lake Camp, the summer Bible camp the church had started the previous year. The camp was on an island in Bay Lake between Garrison and Brainerd in Crow Wing County, Minnesota, about 110 miles northwest of St. Paul and 15 miles east of Brainerd.

The Junior Men's Brotherhood from the church went up early in the season and, with axes, they built hiking trails around the island to make it a better camping experience. However, Marland returned to the camp alone that year because Elmie was expecting their first child – me – and she was ill with pre-eclampsia. Mrs. Friberg, a minister's widow, worked as the camp cook that summer in place of my mother.

On a day in early July, Dad received word at the camp that Elmie had been taken to Bethesda Hospital in St. Paul to induce a premature birth to reduce the risk to her and the baby. My father sped over rough gravel roads toward St. Paul in a borrowed REO automobile only to have a valve-stem break in the motor. He said the motor made an awful noise, but he decided to keep on driving. The date was July 4, 1927.

Dad's medical school connections at that time were helpful. He persuaded a specialist to come in and advise Dr. Olaf Ivar Sohlberg who was in charge of the delivery. The birth apparently was hard on both mother and child because Dad told me that I was unable to breathe on my own.

Because my survival was questionable, Pastor A.W. Knock from First Lutheran Church baptized me the next day in the hospital. Dad's oldest sister, Olga Williams, and Elmie's oldest brother, Alfer Strom, were my baptismal sponsors. In a day or so I got stronger and was able to breathe without oxygen.

During those tense days at the hospital, some of Dad's friends repaired the REO so he was able to return to Bay Lake to continue supervising the camp construction. (Incidentally, the letters REO were the initials of Ransom E. Olds, the founder of the Oldsmobile Motor Company

Baby Jerry, 1927

which later merged into General Motors.) My mother and I spent the rest of the summer at her parents' home at 546 Beau-

The Williams Family, ca. 1931, Marland, Elmie, Jerry and Keith

mont Street in St. Paul.

After my birth, my parents had to find larger living quarters, so they moved to a small house at 614 Erie Street Southeast near the University campus, and soon after that to 90 Malcolm Avenue Southeast in the Prospect Park neighborhood of Minneapolis.

Moving to Cannon Falls

When I was about three years old, my father completed his

medical internship at Bethesda Hospital and began looking for a place to practice medicine and surgery. Dr. O. I. Sohlberg, the doctor who delivered me and had served as Dad's mentor at Bethesda, was a native of Cannon Falls. He drove Dad there to look over the vacant practice of Dr. Alva Conley who had recently passed away as a result of x-ray burns from his new machine. X-ray technology was in its infancy at that time and the danger of exposure was not very well understood. Dad recalled encountering Dr. Conley at Bethesda a few months earlier when he saw this sickly gentleman leaning against a marble post in the lobby of Bethesda Hospital. He went over and asked if he could

be of help, and Dr. Conley told him his sad story of dying of x-ray induced cancer.

Dad told me that he had taken extra coursework in x-ray technology at the University of Minnesota medical school and felt that with proper precautions, he could use Dr. Conley's equipment safely. After Dad was introduced to Dr. Conley's widow, he bought the practice with money he borrowed from his family members.

Elmie, Jerry, Keith, ca. 1931

Marland and Elmie rented a large house on the main street

4

of Cannon Falls. It had three floors and a stairway to an attic – an adventure-filled space. The house had large bay windows from which one could see the whole neighborhood. Because the street in front of our house was quite busy, we kids were not permitted to cross the street to visit the greenhouse with pretty flowers.

Behind our first house lived a girl about my age. Her name was Shirley Roell and her dad owned the local Chevrolet garage. She was the only kid who lived nearby so Shirley and I became good friends. Once I fell off her back porch and broke my right arm, so that gave my dad something to do. We had a dog. I think it was a German shepherd; his name was Chief. From then on, we always had dogs, but only one at a time.

It was probably 1934 when the Minnesota Highway Department and the Federal Highway Administration decided to upgrade the road in front of our house to become U.S. Highway 52 between Cannon Falls, St. Paul, and Rochester. That meant more and faster vehicles would pose a danger for Keith and me.

I remember Dad drove me to school my first day of kindergarten and after that my parents bought a different house in Cannon Falls. This supports what Dad told me not long before he died when I asked why he always took his patients to St. John's Hospital in Red Wing or to Bethesda Hospital in St. Paul. I asked, "Why didn't you take your patients to Rochester?" He said, "Because that was a gravel road."

Our new house was located at the intersection of Mill and Elm streets. There were no street signs then, but as a Boy Scout merit badge project I drew a map of the town surrounding our house, the school, and the church, so I learned the street names. From our house, it was a three-block walk to school and one more block to our church, St. Ansgar's Lutheran.

This house was at the top of Limekiln Hill. Well, not exactly the top, but as high up as the street went. In the winter the city blocked off the cross street at the bottom of the hill so kids could sled down for two full blocks. Some older boys had a bobsled. They could go four blocks – all the way to "downtown."

Limekiln Hill rose a few hundred more feet above our house. At the top were two fascinating things: an abandoned limestone quarry and the city water tank. The water tank was not one of those metal tanks on long steel legs. It was a stone-lined rectangular hole in the ground with a wood shingle roof. The edges of the roof extended down to the ground so we could climb on it, but the door on the end was always locked. The quarry was great fun for playing because it rambled around. It was the perfect place for hide and seek and shooting rubber-band guns.

We made rubber band guns using sticks and rubber strips we cut from old inner tubes we could get free from Lindahl's Tire and Harness Shop. In those days there was a soft rubber inner tube lining the inside of a tire. When a car ran over a nail, the tire and inner tube could be punctured. Often the inner tube could be patched, and the tire restored to use. We rode our bikes or walked to Lindahl's to get the old inner tubes that could no longer be patched.

Chapter 2

MY TWO MOTHERS

Elmie Mildred Strom

My mother, Elmie, died when I was six years old, so most of what I know about her was told to me by my father and others. Elmie Mildred Strom was born on January 21, 1899, in St. Paul. She was the third of six children born to John Henning Strom and his wife Mathilda Johnson. John immigrated from Hova, Sweden in 1888 and worked for the St. Paul fire department most of his adult life. "Tillie" came from Lönashult, Sweden, in 1889. They were married in 1894 in St. Paul.

The parents of my mother and father were acquainted through First Lutheran Church in St. Paul. It is said they thought their children would be a good marriage match.

Elmie's parents had encouraged her to write to Marland while he was serving in France during the war. When he returned from France in February 1919 and they could spend time together, their feelings for each other deepened.

My mother had a good

Marland and Elmie, 1923

mind. When she was twenty, she enrolled in the Lutheran Bible Institute, a two-year degree institution in the basement of First Lutheran Church. In 1923, she graduated from the Academic Department of Minnesota College as class salutatorian.

After the war my father worked as an auto mechanic at a Pure Oil Company station. Elmie wanted to become a missionary. She encouraged Dad to go to medical school so he could accompany her to the mission field as a physician, so he enrolled in the University of Minnesota for undergraduate courses and was later accepted into medical school.

My parents were married on August 11, 1923, in his parents' large flower and vegetable garden at their home at 1530 Burns Avenue in St. Paul. While my father was in medical school, my mother taught eighth grade at her alma mater, Minnesota College. By the time Dad graduated in 1929, my brother, Keith, and I were in the picture. Instead of going to the mission field, my dad took over a general medical-surgical practice in Cannon Falls.

Elmie put her education and missionary zeal to work teaching a women's Bible study at St. Ansgar's Lutheran Church. It was said Pastor Nelson was envious because her classes were better

Elmie & Marilyn shortly before Elmie's death in 1934

attended than his. My sister, Marilyn, was born during that time.

8

My mother died on June 20, 1934, from an infection that resulted from a surgical mishap. My father often lamented that an antibiotic as basic as penicillin might have saved her life, but that miracle drug would not available for therapeutic use until seven years later.

Viola Elizabeth Grisim

While my father, known around town as "Doc Williams," cared for the people of Cannon Falls, we three kids were cared for by a succession of housekeepers until July 14, 1936, when Dad married Viola Elizabeth Grisim. Viola embraced the role of stepmother, and about a year and a half later, she added my brother Roger (we always called him Butch) to the family.

Viola was born on September 10,1906, the third child of Jasper Sovern Grisim and Carolyn "Carrie" Winifred (Phenning) Grisim. She was born at home on the farm, a very common occurrence at that time.

My father met Viola when he was called as the family doctor to the Grisim farm home near Randolph to see their sick daughter. Viola had come home from St. Olaf College in Northfield complaining of pain in her abdomen. A quick examination indicated appendicitis. Dad's usual procedure at the time was to transfer the patient on a stretcher in his car and bring the patient to one of two hospitals for emergency surgery. He could have taken her to Bethesda Hospital in St. Paul where he had interned, or to St. John's Hospital in Red Wing. Because the Grisim family lived only a mile or so west of U.S. Highway 52 and a few miles north of Cannon Falls, the odds are he took her to Bethesda.

Side note: In the 1930s, Highway 52 was called the Capitol Highway because it terminated at the Minnesota state capitol in St. Paul, just a short distance from Bethesda Hospital. South of Cannon Falls, the highway's concrete pavement ended, so Dad seldom took his patients to Rochester until 1934 when the state acquired the gravel roads from the counties to realign and pave them.

Viola recovered nicely from the appendectomy and returned to St. Olaf. She graduated in 1936 with a Bachelor of Music degree, majoring in vocal performance. This is a good place to explain how Viola was able to attend St. Olaf College.

Viola's older sister, Grace, was employed by Frederick Douglas Underwood, the retired president of the Erie Railroad. It was her job to oversee his large country summer home, named Westwood, near Farmington. It was a challenging job for Grace, because it was like operating a small hotel, as Mr. Underwood frequently had overnight guests visiting from the East Coast.

One day Mr. Underwood asked Grace if she could find someone to drive him around the countryside in the afternoons. The idea came to Grace that perhaps Viola could do that job, so after an introduction, Mr. Underwood employed Viola as his chauffer and bought a nice new car for those afternoon excursions.

The following is conjecture on my part, because I didn't have the foresight to ask Viola for details when I was younger. I can imagine this conversation between Mr. Underwood and Viola as they became acquainted during their afternoon drives:

"Viola, why isn't a bright young lady like you enrolled in college?" Her reply undoubtedly was something like, "Because my parents can't afford it." As a result of Viola's first summer working for Mr. Underwood, she was able to enroll at St. Olaf College in 1932 with a full four-year scholarship endowed by Mr. Underwood. She was considered a special student there because of her advanced age – she was 26.

Viola & Frederick Underwood

Viola was blessed with an exceptionally beautiful singing voice. All four years she attended at St. Olaf she sang in the top choir, frequently featured as a soloist. I believe the director, Dr. F. Melius Christiansen, appreciated the strength and maturity of her voice. I was pleased to find this photo of Viola in the St. Olaf archives. She is seated front row center, with F. Melius directly behind her. I was just nine years old when she married Dad, but I remember Viola taking our family to the St. Olaf Christmas festivals every year after that. The St. Olaf Choir always occupied a very special place in her heart.

When Dad began dating Viola, she frequently visited our home in Cannon Falls with several of her classmates. Two of

St. Olaf Choir, Viola Grisim, front row, 7th from left

those young ladies, Evangeline (Haupert) Graf and Marcella (Oldenberg) Von Goertz, were her life-long friends. When they came to our home, they always made us kids very comfortable by showing sincere interest in our hobbies and school achievements.

Dad and Viola were married by Reverend O. Birger Nelson in the living room of our home on April 14, 1936. While they were on their honeymoon, my siblings and I stayed with our Aunt Helen and Uncle Al Strom (my mother's oldest brother) in Mankato. That was a memorable adventure for us because we had never been away from home before. We

Marland & Viola, July 15, 1936

12

had a great time with one of the two neighbor kids whose family owned a player piano with a goodly supply of punched paper recordings.

I recall a family vacation we took to the Dakota Badlands and the Black Hills. That trip was memorable because there was a grasshopper plague and it was before cars had air conditioning, so we had to drive with the windows down in order to get some relief from the heat. When the grasshoppers flew in the front windows Viola caught them and tossed them to us in the back seat.

Viola was a great mother to my siblings and me. I recall how she patiently listened to me recite my memorized confirmation Bible lessons. After I returned from the Navy in July of 1946, I intended to register at the University of Minnesota in electrical engineering, but I was told those classes were already filled with men who had been released from service before me. The regis-

Williams Family- Viola and Marland with Marilyn, Keith and Jerry, ca. 1937

trar told me I should come back the next year.

When I told my parents I could not get into the "U" this year, Viola said, "Instead of wasting a year, I will take you to Northfield tomorrow." I knew "Northfield" meant St. Olaf. Her reasoning was that my first year of classes at "the U" would probably be chemistry, physics, math, and English, and the credits for those subjects would transfer to the University of MN. The St. Olaf College admissions officer said they would accept me on the condition that I find my own housing, because the college had exhausted every possible means to house students with so many men enrolling after WWII. Viola suggested that we visit the library to see if any of the ladies she knew when she was a student were still working there. We found a pastor's widow, Mrs. Johanna Winger, who said she had already agreed to take one boy and if I didn't mind sleeping in double bed with him, we could share the bedroom in her home at 409 North Plum Street, so that is what I did for my first year at St. Olaf.

Viola died on September 11, 1949, from an abscess that developed after she suffered a blood clot in her lung. She and Elmie are both buried in the Williams family plot in Union Cemetery in Maplewood.

I am so grateful to Viola for pointing me toward St. Olaf. I would never have attended that school without her intervention, and I would never have found Lorraine, who would become my first wife, and her twin sister, Florraine, who would eventually be my second wife. Looking back, I can see the Lord was guiding my decisions and shaping my future.

One reason I established the Viola Grisim Williams En-

The Williams Family - Roger, Viola, Marilyn, Keith, Jerry, Marland, ca. 1948

dowed Scholarship in Fine Arts at St. Olaf College was because I did not take the opportunity while she was living to tell her how much I appreciated what she did for me. Viola did so much to shape me into the person that I am now. I am forever grateful for her impact on my life.

Jerry, Keith, Marilyn

Chapter 3

MY CANNON FALLS SCHOOL YEARS

Memories of Kindergarten

Kindergarten in Cannon Falls was a by-product of a special Teacher-Training Program known as Normal Training. Girls who graduated from high school could enroll in a year-long course of study that would prepare graduates to become teachers for rural one-room schools.

Miss Lenora Rudow was their teacher. In the spring "her girls" were our kindergarten teachers for six weeks. A lot of great people came out of those one-room rural schools. After our mother died, several of those girls lived in our house and did housework in exchange for food and lodging. Most of them were farm girls and they knew how to work and cook. After supper, they would wash the dishes and Keith or I would dry. We became good friends with those girls and were always disappointed when they left. Some of those farm girls were from Wisconsin across the Mississippi River from Red Wing.

One day there was a graduation celebration for the kindergarten students. My mother did not arrive, so Miss Rudow said, "Jerry, I'll be your mother today." That worked for me, but I was so disappointed my mother wasn't there. I remember when I got home, she was standing in the back hallway ironing clothes. I told her how disappointed I was that she didn't come to the party. She said, "I didn't know about it!" Just then, as she was ironing one of my shirts, she took a piece of paper from the pocket. It was the invitation to the party. We were both sad. It was my fault for not giving her the invitation. That is one of the few things I can remember about my mother who died shortly afterward in 1934.

Williams Home at 125 East Mill Street, Cannon Falls

Memories of Elementary Grades

First grade. My teacher was Miss Madsen, who I remember for two things. She was the only grade schoolteacher who gave me a "D" on my report card – and it was for music! The second thing was when we were learning to print our names. She sat beside me and explained it would be easier for me to print my nickname, Jerry, instead of Gerald, and that I should know how to do that anyway because all the kids called me Jerry. Then she told me that there are two ways to spell it: girls use a G for the first letter, but boys always use a J. Who would argue with their first grade teacher? They know everything! So, it was J-E-R-R-Y for me from then on.

Second grade. My teacher was Miss Swanson. She seemed kind of like a mother to me after losing my birth mother. Perhaps Miss Swanson saw that as her special responsibility for me. I really liked her. She came back to visit our class when we were in junior high. Wow, what a doll! At that time, she was on the Broadway stage in New York. I would not have recognized her that day until she told us who she was. I wish I could talk to her now.

Third grade. My teacher was Miss Worra. She was strict but not as strict as the next one.

Fourth grade. My teacher was Miss Julia Miller. She was very strict and carried a wooden ruler, but we learned a lot from her. The two subjects I best remember learning are multiplication tables and the geography of the Belgian Congo. There was a brother and sister in my class who kept having to repeat it: Lois and Curtis Rapp. They were at least a foot taller than me. I suspect now they might have had ADHD or a vision problem. In 1936, those things were not identified like they are now. My brother, Keith, my sister, Marilyn, and my half-brother, Roger, also had Miss Miller as their 4th grade teacher. Apparently, teaching 4th grade in Cannon Falls was her life's career.

Fifth grade. Miss Wyman was my teacher. I liked her very much and got good grades from her. That was the year I started learning to play my Uncle Stanley's alto saxophone in the school band. I was excused from class once each week for a private lesson with Mr. Paul Heltne, our band director.

Sixth grade. My teacher was Miss Patricia O'Loughlin. She was a favorite of mine. She treated me as if I was more mature than the others.

Memories of Junior and Senior High School

When I was in junior high, George Kaisersatt, a Minnesota State Highway Patrolman, organized the State School Patrol program in Cannon Falls. Officer Kaisersatt was a good friend of my father as the result of frequently working side-by-side at automobile accidents. Our Cannon Falls School Patrol was sponsored by the American Legion Post in Cannon Falls. That was while my father was the Post Commander so George knew where he could get support.

At noon, those of us selected to be crossing guards were excused from school a few minutes early so we could pick up our equipment and hurry to our assigned street crossings. After

Crossing Guard, Jerry top left

all the kids had come through our intersections on their way home for lunch, we would run home, eat quickly and be back on duty to get the kids safely across the street and on their way to school again. Fortunately, my assigned intersection was only two blocks from my home, but the last block was up a steep hill to our house. I developed really strong legs that still carry me well today. That was also true for my brother and sister.

One of my father's most prized possessions was the brass life membership card awarded to him by the Minnesota State Highway Patrol Officers Association. He always carried it, and it came in handy when he was stopped for speeding in his Oldsmobile Toronado. Because of its color and his fast driving, the

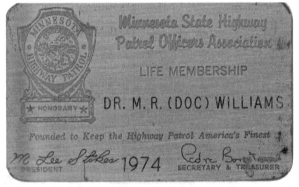

Marland's brass State Patrol Life Membership

highway patrol nicknamed it the "white tornado."

Seventh grade. My math teacher was Mr. Walter Gohman. He became our Boy Scout Master after Alton Schneider moved. The way he taught geometry made sense to me and I still like and remember it. Perhaps it was because I could visualize those geometric objects.

Eighth grade. Our home room teacher was Miss Maude Desso. She stressed reading books, giving book reports, and Palmer Method penmanship. I wish she could see my papers now. When I was in her class my papers were a mess. I was a perfectionist then, but after many erasures my papers looked awful. I hated to turn them in that way, but there wasn't time for re-writing. What a difference a word processor makes for writing compositions now! My penmanship was bad then, but not as bad as that of my father, the doctor.

My junior high biology teacher was Mr. Urdahl. He really knew the subject and was always well-prepared.

My junior high shop teacher was Mr. William Nigg. He was a favorite teacher of mine – a good science teacher, a good shop teacher, and just a very nice person. He was unmarried while in Cannon Falls, but he married soon after he moved to Mankato. I believe he became the school superintendent there.

One evening in the 1970s while living in Edina, our family went out for supper to Bridgeman's restaurant in Bloomington. Another family walked in as we were finishing our meal. I said to my family, "You will have to excuse me because I believe that I know the man who just came in with his family." As I approached their table, I started to say, "I'm Jerry..." Mr. Nigg interrupted me and said, "You're Jerry Williams, right?" I said, "Yes!" and then one of his sons chuckled and said, "This happens to us all the time." We had a great visit; what an incredible experience! He had not seen me for at least twenty or twenty-five years, when I was in high school. Now here he was, the father of three teenagers.

My senior high shop teacher was Alton Schneider. He also was our scoutmaster. He was very good. My favorite class from him was engineering drawing. I still have some of my first drawings. When I finished that class, I wanted to become a drafts-man because I thought they were same as engineers. I later learned the draftsman's job was to redraw the engineer's sketch or drawing to make it more legible and more complete in detail. They did not develop or design anything, so my goal changed to becoming an engineer.

I really appreciated my men teachers. They were wonderful male role models for me. Our father spent so little time with us kids that we only saw him as the boss of our home and occasion-ally as our doctor, but it seemed to us that we had to be really sick for that to materialize. If we needed medicine, we were treated with free samples from his black bag, so we thought we must not be very sick.

In my senior year of high school, Mr. Bill Anderson, the football coach, asked me to join the team because they were short of players. I did so because so many of my friends played on the team. It was good for me because I wasn't getting much exercise in our basement building model airplanes and repair-ing radios for the townspeople. Mr. Anderson worked us hard and I built up some muscle, but it didn't do us much good as a team because we had a terrible season. He had us line up in the single-wing formation. The best players on our team wanted to use the new T-formation that most of our opponents used, but Mr. Anderson didn't agree. We won two, tied one and lost four. Pine Island beat us 75 to zero. That was really humiliating! I still remember the Kenyon game because my hands were so cold that the referee loaned me his gloves. Good guy!

Our senior class play, *Our Town* by Thornton Wilder, was the

Front Row: Evalyn Schwartau, Elrene Haggstrom, Beulah Skaro, Leora Anderson, Arline Holmes, Dorothy Baird, Jean Anderson, Deloris Pagel, Doris Soule, Arlene Robinson, Elva Chellson. Second Row: Donald Gustafson, Hamline Johnson, Lloyd Schultz, Ingroy Loven, Wayne Erickson, Gerald Williams, Keith Danielson, LeRoy Young, William Hanson. Third Row: Phyllis VanGuilder, Peter Nelson, Stanley Lindholm, Mildred Hernke, Richard Gustafson, Clarence Kappedahl, Robert Nelson, Robert Lee, Miss Connole, Miss Anderson. Back Row: Mr. Hansen (Director), Dena Westvik, Arnold Dabelow, Robert O'Gorman, Lee Hanson, Clifford Kappedahl, Miss Nelson.

Cannon Falls High School Class Play, "Our Town"

first time I had a speaking part in a stage play. I was cast in the
role of Howie Newsome, the friendly milkman, who in those
days, delivered milk in bottles to homes. That is the way it was
done at our home too, but we had two milkmen. Mr. Mattson
delivered milk to the front door and Melvin Johnson delivered
it to the back door. That was because both men's families were
patients of our father and he felt obligated to patronize both.
Milk came in re-useable glass quart bottles sealed with a round
paperboard disk. If it was really cold outside, the milk would
freeze if left outside too long. It would expand and push the top
up an inch or so. It looked cute. The milk was not homogenized
at that time, so the cream would rise to the top. That was called
top milk and we saved it to put on our cereal because it tasted

23

better than the residual milk.

Working for Allen Peter While in High School

My chief hobby was building and flying model airplanes, a hobby I really enjoyed and shared with several other classmates in school. My dad encouraged me in that hobby because my hands were a bit shaky. He thought building model airplanes would help to steady my hands. It didn't. Instead I just became very adept at finding assembly techniques to compensate for my unsteady hands. But I realize retrospec-

Jerry built many model airplanes

tively my father had a deep interest in seeing that my spare time was well spent, because those interests did keep me off the street.

When I was a lad of fourteen or so, my parents gave me a Christmas gift of an electronics kit from Allied Radio Corporation in Chicago. That radio kit opened the door to a fascinating new world of interest. It was a world far more complex and intriguing to me than model airplanes.

During that time, our father thought we should improve the basement by putting in more lighting and electrical outlets, so he hired an electrician. He could have easily done it himself but during the World War II years, he was seeing patients night and day and did not have the time for that task. The electrician for the job was Allen Peter who was raised on a farm near Randolph.

Allen noticed my radio kit activity and asked if I would be interested in working for him in his shop after school hours. He was extremely busy as a result of the war. He was the only electrician in town and was not in his shop much of the day because he was out wiring farm buildings that never had electricity before. The REA (Rural Electrification Agency) was installing power lines to the farms as fast as possible to increase production of farm produce to aid the war effort.

Allen shared a building with a certified public accountant/ justice of the peace, and a radio repairman. Those two men did their best to help folks in Allen's absence from the shop, but mostly they just took in repairs and sold a few light bulbs, fuses and switches. Allen wanted me to do more that that. I worked for him from 4:00 to 6:00 after school on weekdays and all day on Saturdays.

On Saturdays, he taught me how to repair toasters, flat-irons, floor and table lamps, and kitchen mixers. From there, my training went on to small gasoline engines for washing machines and well pumps. I even learned how to replace the bearings in electric motors.

In the summer months I went with him out to the farms and learned how to wire cow barns, bathrooms, and bedrooms. It was a wonderful education. At the end of a day in the country, Allen taught me how to drive his 1936 Chevrolet coupe that had a huge trunk to carry all his tools and small electrical parts.

Big stuff like conduit went up top, tied to car-top carriers. Allen was a great teacher. When I had his car under control, he would explain different kinds of wiring circuits to me.

The most unusual trip I took with Allen was to Minneapolis to pick up wiring supplies needed for an upcoming job. When Allen picked me up at our home that morning, I saw he had his one-year-old daughter in the car. My job that day was to hold her in my lap and keep her amused while her mother was at work at Scofield's drug store. Little Julie and I got along very well.

I learned a lot from Allen, like sometimes, if a project isn't going well, you just have to "tough it out" and "double down."

The U.S. Navy Interrupts My Education

In December of my senior year in high school, I enlisted in the U.S. Navy, so I was not present for the graduation ceremony in the spring. My brother, Keith, picked up my yearbook and gathered some autographs for me. My parents stepped up to receive my diploma plus a few awards, and it was announced I was the honorary salutatorian. Just before that, I had been home on a short leave in the spring of 1944, and that was when some pictures

Jerry on the football team, Cannon Falls High School yearbook, 1944

were being taken for the yearbook. That explains why I was wearing my sailor uniform in the yearbook and I didn't bother to put on my shoulder pads for the football picture, which is why I look so round-shouldered compared to the other players. How did I come to play football? There were only six men in our senior class – the coach begged me to play!

Chapter 4

MY NAVY YEARS
DECEMBER 11, 1944 TO JULY 5, 1946

**Transforming a High School Kid
into a Naval Electronic Technician**

In 1944, the United States was at war with Germany in Europe and Japan in the Pacific. All young men, when they reached seventeen years of age, were called into the U.S. Army as soon as they graduated from high school. That meant I would be eligible for the draft on my seventeenth birthday on July fourth that year. All eligible older men had long since been drafted.

My father served in the Army during World War I as a seventeen-year-old. He saw some terrible battle scenes in France, and had a rough go of it, sleeping in barns, open fields and forests, and having to beg for food from French civilian families. He did not want to see me drafted into the Army. Based on his war experience sailing to and from France, Dad saw that sailors had clean, comfortable places to sleep and better food to eat than the soldiers in the Army.

The Navy had recently retrofitted their older vessels with newly available equipment called RADAR, (Radio Detection and Ranging) and SONAR (Sound Navigation and Ranging). This created a sudden need for electronics technicians because no one aboard those ships had been trained to maintain this sophisticated new equipment.

At that time my father was the commander of the American Legion post in Cannon Falls, so he became aware the Navy was looking for men who were skilled in electronics to maintain the shipboard equipment. During my high school years, I had acquired a working knowledge of radio by repairing radio receivers for the townspeople after Clair Johnson, the only remaining local radio serviceman, was drafted. Before leaving for the Army, Clair gave me several evenings of instruction on how to use his test equipment.

I recall one October evening Dad had invited a Navy recruiting officer to our home for dinner. The recruiter explained the Navy's radio technician training program to me and my parents. After dinner, he pulled from his brief case an examination called the "Eddy Test." He said if I passed the test, I would be considered qualified to enlist in the radio technician program after I finished high school in June. In a few weeks, I received a notice in the mail that I had passed the test.

In early December, the recruiter called my father and told him they would like to have me report to Fort Snelling in Minneapolis on December 10th for a physical examination to be certain that I was in satisfactory health to serve in the Navy.

Dad drove me up to Fort Snelling, said goodbye, and dropped me off. I had no difficulty passing the physical exam. However, to my surprise and dismay, I was told that instead of going home to finish high school, I was to report to the Federal Building in downtown Minneapolis at 8:30 the next morning to be sworn into the U.S. Navy.

It was almost Christmas and I hadn't finished high school

yet. What had my dad gotten me into? I called home and asked him what I should do. Dad suggested I could stay overnight with Grandma Williams in St. Paul, and after that, I should just do as I was told.

I called Grandma and she told me how to get to her house. I had never ridden the streetcars on my own before so that was a new adventure. My aunts, Olga and Jewell, were very upset with my father, their brother, for getting me into the situation where I could not be home for Christmas or graduate from high school, and they called to tell him so. As I recall, he responded that he had enlisted in the Army at the same age and it would be a good experience for me.

I'm in the Navy Now!

The next day at the Federal Building I was told that I would be on the afternoon train to Great Lakes Naval Station for basic training, commonly known as boot camp. "Great Mistakes," as it was un-affectionately called, was just north of Chicago on the west shore of Lake Michigan. I was also told I would be in charge of the twenty-five-man contingent traveling there. When I asked, "Why me?" they replied that despite my age, I looked like the recruit best able to handle

Jerry Williams, 1944

30

that responsibility.

The Chicago Northwestern Railway station was just a few blocks walk from the Federal Building, and before I knew it, my contingent was on its way. The 400-mile trip took about seven hours and included dinner in the dining car. We arrived at Great Lakes after dark and were quickly ushered to temporary sleeping quarters.

Great Lakes Naval Training Station

The following day we were given another physical exam and received vaccinations for various diseases including scarlet fever. (Since scarlet fever is caused by bacteria, it's now known that vaccinations are not useful, but they were given to recruits at that time.) The most memorable part of the physical was seeing blood drawn from my forearm into huge syringes. I was startled to see my blood was not red, but a bluish-purple. It was such a surprise that I instantly weakened and asked for a drink of water. The next thing I knew, two fellows were holding me up in the air by my ankles, stark naked! I had fainted for the first time in my life. It would not be the last.

Next, we were issued our clothing, both "blues" and "whites," as well as dungarees (blue jeans to landlubbers). It took me quite a while to figure out my shoe size using a self-fitting trial-and-error process because I had never paid any attention to that as a kid. The store clerks had always worked that out.

I was assigned to Company 2278. The company was made up entirely of recruits like me who had enlisted in the Radio Technician (RT) Training program. I was one of the youngest in the company. Many of the fellows had been pulled out of college, but a few were already experienced graduate engineers working in industry. We were immediately given the rank of Seaman 1st Class instead of having to begin as Apprentice Seamen. Sailors normally progress upward from Apprentice Seaman to Seaman 2nd Class and then to Seaman 1st Class after two or three more years at sea. Beginning as Seaman 1st Class (RT) was nice recognition and also gave us a bit higher pay. As I recall, we were paid $66 each month. I had never earned that much before, so that seemed like a lot of money.

At Great Lakes, we learned to march, work in the mess hall, stand guard duty in the dark of the night, shovel coal into the stoker that heated our barracks, scrub floors, clean toilets, and a little bit about knot-tying. We were subjected to strenuous gymnastic exercises, including diving off high boards to simulate jumping off a ship, and some life-saving techniques.

Every night they made us use steel wool to clean the wooden floor in our barracks on our hands and knees until our black heel marks were no longer visible. That was a terrible job – hard on my hands and very dusty, and I developed a sinus infection that was terribly painful. Whether that infection was created by the steel wool dust or from a bad fall that I took in gymnastics, landing on the top of my head, I'll never know. I spent hours in sick bay with cotton swabs stuck up my nostrils into the sinus cavities. One day in my misery, I called home to talk to Dad. He was aware of a Navy nurse from Cannon Falls who was stationed at Great Lakes and he contacted her. Madeline Larson, whose sister, Yvonne, was one of my school classmates, found me and saw that I got treatment to help me, as well as some pain medication. To me, she was an angel sent from heaven whose kindness I have never forgotten.

In late January we were told our training would be cut short because the fleet was desperate for radio technicians. The next day we were sent to the first of the three schools that comprised the forty-four-week Radio Technician curriculum. Instead of the usual twelve weeks of boot camp we had only six. One of the things we missed was rifle train-

Doodlebug (Marty Bernard photo, used with permission)

ing. The irony of that will come later. As I recall we had a few days off and discovered military service personnel could ride the trains for free, so I took the Hiawatha, one of the early railroad streamliners, from Chicago to Red Wing. From there I caught a small train called the Doodlebug. The first car of the Doodlebug had its own diesel engine and served as the baggage and mail car. It pulled just one passenger car and ran from Red Wing to Randolph, with a brief stop at Cannon Falls. Fortunately, its schedule meshed well with the Hiawatha line. I became well acquainted with that schedule over the next year.

The RT program was the brainchild of retired Navy Captain William C. Eddy, which explains the name of the entrance exam I took that night at home. He had been a young officer but was medically retired from the Navy sometime before the war. When the Japanese attacked Pearl Harbor on December 7, 1941, Mr. Eddy was pioneering television broadcasting for the Balaban & Katz division of Paramount Pictures in Chicago. With great foresight he recognized a critical need to train radio and radar technicians to maintain the Navy's electronic equipment. He volunteered his B&K staff and facilities in Chicago for that purpose. The Navy quickly accepted his offer and the RT training program was soon created and underway.

There were three phases to the program. The first phase was called Pre-Radio and consisted of three and a half weeks of algebra, basic electricity, and shop practice. That phase also served to weed out those who lacked the necessary aptitude, knowledge, or skills to complete the program.

Wright Junior College, Chicago

My Pre-Radio training took place at Wright Junior College, located on Austin Boulevard on the west edge of Chicago. The Navy took over the entire facility enabling us to live and study there around the clock. We had instruction about ten hours a day, with classes in the morning, afternoon, and evening after supper. We studied together. We ate together in the school cafeteria. We slept together in triple-decker bunk beds in the gymnasium. Those few hours of sleep were the only interruption in our studies.

Unfortunately, I became very ill with scarlet fever while I was there, so I was sent back to the hospital at Great Lakes. There were hundreds of us there suffering from this miserable disease caused by streptococcus bacteria. I was in a ward with about fifty other men. It was a traumatic experience because someone died almost every day.

After the war, when I was a passenger on a commercial airliner, the man seated next to me said he had been a hospital corpsman at Great Lakes during that time. He shared that the Navy ultimately realized they had received a bad batch of scarlet fever vaccine. Most likely the bad vaccine I received at Great Lakes a few weeks before combined with the stressful life at Wright Junior College had weakened my body enough to succumb to the disease.

Newly available penicillin was the medication the doctors chose to use to combat the disease. It was administered with a shot into our rumps several times a day by attractive young nurses. They were sympathetic which helped us tolerate the pain. It took me four weeks to recover. I was returned to Wright to complete the Pre-Radio training but suffered a relapse after a few days and was sent back to Great Lakes for a short time until I was fully recovered. Upon my return to Wright I had to resume training with a new group of men, but that turned out to be a blessing because some of them were graduate electrical engineers. They accepted and coached me, so I was able to pass the final exam. I was thrilled to successfully complete that first phase, because I had not finished all of the required math and science classes in high school.

Gulfport, Mississippi

The next twelve-week phase of our training program was called Primary Elementary Electricity & Radio Materiel (EE & RM). We were given a choice of where we would do that phase of training. I opted to go to Gulfport, Mississippi, since I had never been in a southern state. This phase of the program was just as rigorous as the first, but much more interesting. It was half theory and half practical shop work. I enjoyed the practical activities during which we made technical drawings, built a one-tube radio, including the sheet metal chassis, and learned how to use a variety of test equipment.

Jerry Williams, 1945

We slept in Quonset huts, about twenty-four men to a hut. Of course, we did our own laundry – a learning experience for me. We scrubbed our clothes on wooden tables outside and rinsed them in buckets of water. The bright sunshine did the bleaching and drying. The warm weather was a real treat and made Gulfport a very pleasant experience. I arrived there in April and left on June 22nd – an ideal time of year to be in Mississippi. There were frequent rain showers, but they didn't last long, and the water quickly filtered down through the barren sand. Raised boardwalks between the buildings kept our shoes clean and dry.

Like in the Pre-Radio phase, we had class sessions morning, afternoon, and evening, interrupted only for meals and PT (physical training). It was a good place to rebuild my strength from the illness of a few weeks earlier. I enjoyed my fellow classmates, most of whom were several years older than me. One of those fellows, Jim Wynn, slept above me. He had been a design engineer for RCA in Camden, New Jersey. Jim was very generous with his spare time, helping me to understand the complexities of electronic theory.

Gulfport was only a short distance from Biloxi, Mississippi, the location of Keesler Air Force Base. While we were there, the Air Force received its first Boeing B-29s, the new long-range bomber developed to replace the B-17. When the B-29s took off from Keesler AFB, they flew right over Gulfport Naval Station at just a few hundred feet above us. They were spectacular.

The townspeople of Gulfport were very friendly. On the weekends we went into town to see a movie, get something different to eat, or write letters and dance at the USO (United Service Organization). The time at Gulfport passed quickly. I have a graduation certificate that said I ranked 149th in my class of 215. I was satisfied with that, considering my young age and inexperience.

While I was in Gulfport, two memorable events occurred that I still associate with that place. On April 12, 1945, President Franklin Roosevelt died and was succeeded by Harry S. Truman. Just a few weeks later, on May 8th, the world rejoiced upon the signing of the armistice in Europe, ending that phase of the war. That day is commonly known as VE Day (Victory in Europe Day). But, as I recall, the celebration was somewhat tempered, because America still had to defeat the Japanese before any of us could think about going home.

Navy Pier, Chicago

The final phase of our training was a six-month course called "Secondary" (Advanced Radio Material). For that, we were offered a choice of two equipment categories: airborne electronics or shipboard electronics, and we had a choice of training locations. My first choice was Navy Pier on the shore of Lake Michigan within walking distance of downtown Chicago. I chose that place mainly because it was the closest location to my home in Cannon Falls. My alternative choice was Treasure Island in San Francisco Bay, a location with which I would later become acquainted, but not by choice.

The training at Navy Pier was mostly hands-on application

Navy Pier, Chicago

with the equipment we could typically expect to find on board ship. In the morning our instructors taught the circuit theory of a specific piece of equipment. In the afternoon we would go to the lab and learn to operate it. Once we had it operating, our instructor would introduce a series of "troubles" behind our backs. Working in teams of three or four, we were required to diagnose and isolate the problems. I excelled in that problem-solving part of our training, probably because of my past experience with diagnosing broken radios in Cannon Falls.

Midway through our training at Navy Pier, the Navy changed our designation from Radio Technician's Mate to Electronic Technician's Mate. They realized that radio equipment was only a small portion of the repertoire of equipment that we were being trained to maintain. Sometime along the way, I had earned the rank of RT 3rd Class, which was then changed to ETM 3rd Class. Those are petty officer ratings, the first step above Seaman 1st Class.

With my promotion to Radio Technician 3rd Class, I also got a pay increase. That gave me a feeling of great wealth. I could almost buy anything I wanted! Instead, I opted to have a fifty dollar war bond deducted from my pay each month and sent home so I wouldn't spend it all.

Life in Chicago was enjoyable. Military service personnel could ride the streetcars and elevated trains free of charge. There were two movie theatres in "the Loop" − mind-boggling to a kid from Cannon Falls. The Oriental and the Chicago Theaters both had stage shows that preceded the movies, and always with a big band playing music. Seeing and hearing the big bands of Guy Lombardo, Wayne King, Sammy Kaye, Duke Ellington, Harry James, Les Brown, and the Jimmy and Tommy Dorsey was a great treat. I also spent time at the Allied Radio store, the place from which I had mail-ordered parts when I was in Cannon Falls. For diversion, several of us visited the flea market on Maxwell Street in the heart of the Jewish ghetto where one could buy almost anything, despite the scarcities created by the war.

Whenever we had a long weekend, I rode the Hiawatha from downtown Chicago to Red Wing and then caught the Doodlebug to Cannon Falls to enjoy a nice visit at home. Frequently I encountered acquaintances from Red Wing on the train returning to Chicago. I had known those fellows from our district Boy Scout activities, so the trip back to Chicago never felt lonely. One of the Red Wing boys was in my same training program at Navy Pier, but he was in a different company.

Some strong friendships developed within Company 201 at Navy Pier. I corresponded with a few of those fellows for several years after the war, but eventually we lost touch. I did reconnect by mail with Don Wonderly from Dayton, Ohio.

Navy Pier also served as a base for a small aircraft carrier used for training pilots. The carrier departed each morning for training exercises without aircraft on board. Pilots from the Glenview Naval Air Station did practice landings and takeoffs from this small carrier. I think it was a converted ore boat. Occasionally, when the carrier returned in late afternoon, there would be an airplane on deck that was unfit to fly again. A crane on the dock would remove the wreckage. We could only imagine what had happened.

While in Chicago, another historic event occurred. On September 2, 1945, the Japanese signed surrender documents aboard the USS Missouri. In celebration, we were released from classes to go on liberty. Needless to say, we all headed for downtown Chicago where the streets were jammed with people hugging and kissing – especially soldiers and sailors out on the street. There was a great outpouring of emotion, knowing the war was over at last, and we could look forward to getting on with our lives.

But my tour of duty in the Navy wasn't finished yet. The first men to go home would be those who had served the longest. Those of us who had joined more recently would have to be part of an orderly shutdown of the war effort. I completed my training at Navy Pier on February 1, 1946. In recognition of our good grades and in preparation for sending us off to sea duty, we were promoted to ETM 2/C and given a pay raise to $78 per month.

I was able to take a few days off before traveling independently to San Francisco where I would be assigned to a ship. Officially, it was called "a delay en route." I went home to Cannon Falls for a few days and connected with Bob Lee, one of my high school classmates who was serving in the U.S. Merchant Marine. We rode the train together to San Francisco where he was to meet his merchant ship. It was quite an experience for two eighteen-year-olds to travel unaccompanied halfway across the country.

41

USS *Artemis*

USS *Artemis*, AKA 21

I reported the next day to Treasure Island in San Francisco Bay. From there I was sent to a naval base near Richmond, California. After a few days there I was assigned to the USS *Artemis*, designated AKA-21. When I first saw the ship from the landing boat, I thought she was beautiful. She was so big! The *Artemis* had been built in 1944 at the Walsh-Kaiser shipyards in Providence, Rhode Island. She was 426 feet long and 58 feet wide. I did not know that instead of having the customary "V" hull of a seagoing vessel, it had a flat bottom that wasn't evident above the water line. I learned that AKA was an acronym for Amphibious Kargo Attack. These ships were designed to operate in shallow water and built to support landing attacks. Once at sea, the vessel had a continual roll that contributed readily to seasickness.

Upon boarding the ship, I was introduced to Lieutenant Junior Grade Collins. He was the communications officer and I was assigned to his group known as N Company (N for navigation). He informed me that he and I were the only Navy reservists on the ship. All the others were "career Navy" men – in it for the long haul. We were the underdogs.

When the ship had docked in San Francisco a few days earlier, all of the men who were not USN (career Navy) had disembarked and the ship was re-staffed. To the best of my knowledge, there were no ETM's who were career Navy, so the Navy had no choice but to assign reservist ETM's like me to the fleet at that time. Mr. Collins also said that as long as I kept everything running smoothly, there was no need for me to report to him on a daily basis.

On the day I came aboard the Artemis, there were two radio technicians anxious to get off. They had been aboard on her previous mission and were scheduled for discharge. They gave me a very brief indoctrination to my job. As I recall, it was less than an hour. Included in my indoctrination were two surprises for which my year of training had not prepared me.

First, they informed me that while the ship was docking or getting underway, it was my job to operate the engine room telegraph (ERT). That sounded technical and appropriate until I was shown the device located on the bridge. It had only two brass handles with pointers that indicated port and starboard (left and right) engine speeds – no electronics! It turned out the ERT didn't really control the speeds. In the engine room there was another pair of dials with pointers that moved as I moved my levers telling the engine room crew to adjust the speed of the engines accordingly. All I had to do was set the pointers at the speed the captain or pilot asked for. Then I was to respond verbally with something like, "Aye, aye, Sir, all engines ahead FULL, SIR!" Being on the ship's bridge was a special treat though, because I could see first-hand what was happening on our ship.

The second job surprise came when the departing technicians handed me a .45 caliber automatic pistol – me, a sailor who never received any rifle training in boot camp! They told me I was the Guard Mail Petty Officer. That job turned out to be kind of a nice perk. They explained that whenever the ship arrived in a port or harbor, there were three sailors who would leave the ship together every weekday morning. One man was assigned to pick up the U.S. mail for the crew members aboard the ship. The second man picked up the movie to be shown on the ship that night. My job was to pick up the official Navy mail for the ship and deliver it to the executive officer when we returned. For this purpose, I was given a conspicuous leather pouch. Having never been taught how to fire a handgun, I prayed I would never be faced with the need to defend myself. I probably would have shot myself in the foot or had the gun grabbed from my trembling hand.

When we were anchored in Pearl Harbor, the mail job didn't take very long. But when we were anchored offshore, we would be taken by boat to shore and not picked up until later in the day, so we had a lot of spare time in places like San Francisco. I got to see a lot of movies and shops then.

Back to California

Apparently, there was something wrong with our ship when I first came aboard. We sailed northward in San Francisco Bay to Richmond where the Artemis was put into dry dock for repairs. That gave me time to go over all of the equipment for which I was responsible. I soon discovered the two RT's who had left the ship before me had not done a very good job of maintenance. A lot of the equipment was inoperable. I fixed what I could with the parts available on board and developed a shopping list of needed parts. As I recall, I had to chase around the Bay Area to various naval bases to get replacement parts.

My equipment responsibility included two 500-watt radio transmitters and four radio receivers in the radio room. On the bridge there was a depth finder and two transceivers used for communicating with our landing craft. We also had two radar systems: an SG navigational radar and an SC air-search radar. While the radar viewing displays were located in the radar room, their related transmitters were in compartments at the base of the forward and aft masts. I was also responsible for maintaining and operating the movie projector and record player.

The ships and crews anchored in San Francisco Bay were routinely called upon to supply teams of two men to work nights as shore patrol in the San Francisco and Oakland areas. Presumably, that was because other men from those vessels roamed the streets, bars, and restaurants. One night I was assigned to that duty and it was a real eye opener for a naïve eighteen-year-old kid from a small town in Minnesota. My mate and I were given special identifying belts and Billy clubs and assigned to patrol the BART (Bay Area Rapid Transit) Station in San Francisco. Our principal task was to watch for intoxicated sailors and return them to their ships. In a few instances we had to escort the disorderly ones to the Treasure Island brig. Treasure Island lies beneath the midpoint of the San Francisco-Oakland Bay Bridge. It was built in 1939 for the Golden Gate International Exposition by excavating soil from the bottom of the bay.

Our ship's next stop was the China Lake Munitions Base where we took on a full load of explosive ordnance. Our mission was to haul the ammunition to the Bikini Atoll in the Marshall Islands. These munitions were to be placed aboard old Navy vessels destined as targets for the atom bomb test in June. Needless to say, there were strict smoking regulations aboard our ship, and we had only a half-crew aboard: 110 men and eight officers. At the time we were told it was because of a scarcity of personnel. I wonder in retrospect if it was a precaution to minimize the loss of life in case of an accident. I learned later that there had been a gigantic explosion at the China Lake base that literally wiped the base off the map and killed a lot of people.

Underway to Pearl Harbor

As we sailed westward into the Pacific toward our intermediate stop at Pearl Harbor, I was at my ERT (Emergency Response Tactical) station on the bridge for the first time. It was fascinating to be there – to watch the bow of the ship rhythmically rise above and fall below the horizon until I realized watching this was making me seasick. As soon as I was relieved from duty, I went below to my bunk.

No sooner had I settled in and begun to relax when I felt a tap on my shoulder. It was one of the radar operators telling me that our navigational radar had stopped working. I was not yet acquainted with the SG radar's transmitter location, so the radar operator had to show me where the equipment was located. Unfortunately, it was inside a small compartment at the base of the forward mast where the bow of the ship was rising, falling, rolling, rising, falling, rolling more than a few feet with each wave we encountered.

At that point I didn't know if I could handle the task or not because I was so nauseous, but the radar operators were nice guys with a lot of sailing experience. They brought me some strong black coffee and dry toast which settled my stomach very quickly. After that, it didn't take me long to find the magnetron (the main power tube) had failed. Fortunately, there was a spare right there, so in a short time the radar was back up and operational, and I looked pretty good to those guys. The "kid sailor" had proven himself.

On our way to Hawaii, the ship split a seam where the diesel fuel was stored so it left a nasty trail of leaked fuel across the Pacific. There wasn't anything to be done about it until we got to Pearl Harbor. Once there, the ship was immediately put into dry dock again. By the time they got the water pumped out of the dry dock, there was a film of oil all over the concrete walls and bottom surface. As I recall, it took almost two weeks to get the leak repaired and everything cleaned off of the vessel and the dock.

My first glimpse of Hawaii was Pearl Harbor. Honolulu was

only seven or eight miles distant and we had a lot of free time to visit the city. The bus ride into town went through field after field of pineapples. My favorite meal in town was baked ham glazed with some of that sweet pineapple. What a treat! There was an opportunity to have my hair cut by a real barber instead of our ship's part-timer. The barbers in Honolulu were young Hawaiian girls, which made it an even more enjoyable experience. Seeing Diamond Head in the distance at the end of a long, clear sandy beach was quite a contrast to some decades later when Lorraine and I visited the island and it was at the end of a monotonous string of hotels along Waikiki beach.

Bob Roush RM 2nd Class and Jerry Williams, Honolulu

I used that stopover at Pearl Harbor to re-supply my radio room with needed spare parts. The main radio room was on the top deck, just a few steps aft of the bridge. "My" radio room – the emergency radio room – was on the fantail of the ship. I had that space all to myself and I became quite possessive of it. This was where my test equipment and spare parts were kept. I had a small workbench there with a three-inch Triumph oscilloscope that I had been trained to use at Gulfport. At that time, that oscilloscope and a frequency meter were the most sophisticated pieces of test equipment aboard the Navy's ships. There was

48

also a 250-watt emergency radio transmitter there. It was about the size of a refrigerator and was never used while I was aboard.

The fantail is the large, open deck area at the stern of a vessel. There was a five-inch cannon there that was used a few times for practice drills. In the evening, the projector was set up there to show movies, and it was the only time and place the guys were permitted to smoke during our voyage. I made some changes to the circuits in the ship's record player to improve the sound that was piped over loudspeakers on the fantail. In the evenings, I served as the disc jockey who spun records from "My Radio Room."

While at Pearl Harbor, additional supplies were loaded aboard the ship, but the deck officer chose to use the cranes on the dock instead of the ship's booms. That meant the ship's long-wire antennas, which stretched between the yardarms of the two masts had to be dropped down onto the deck because the dock cranes were too tall to pass underneath them. The antennas were woven steel wire cables about half-inch in diameter. After several years of exposure to salt spray they had become rusty and frayed.

I was dismayed when the executive officer decided to put out to sea before we had time to put those antenna cables back in

Jerry Williams, 1946

49

place, because I was informed that I would be responsible for that job with some help from his deck crew after we were underway. Putting them back up meant I had to climb up the forward mast with a rope line tied to the antennas and feed the rope line and antenna cables through pulleys at the ends of the yard arm, one cable at a time. Shinnying out about eight feet on the yardarm while the ship was rolling from side to side and pitching up and down was not my idea of fun. Perhaps you, the reader, can visualize my peril from the picture of the ship. To make it even more exciting, the rusted cables and pulleys did not roll smoothly. One of the seamen below used a winch to pull the cables into position, but each time the pulleys or antennas got hung up on rusty spots, the yardarm on which I was perched would make a sharp jerk until the cable came loose. While all this was going on, I could look down and watch the sea appear below me as the ship rolled, first on my left and then on my right. The two yardarms were 110 feet above the water. That would have been a really high dive! I was glad I was too busy to think of the consequences.

Bikini Atoll

Bikini Atoll is a small crescent-shaped island that the U.S. government seized from the natives. They were forced to relocate to another island some forty miles away – a very cruel thing to do to them. The new island's residents considered the transplanted Bikini natives to be intruders because they had no previous association.

Bikini's crescent shape formed a natural harbor that offered sheltered anchorage for the fleet of ships that were to be destroyed by exploding an atomic bomb above them. The United States was determined to conduct this test to learn the consequences to a whole fleet if an A-bomb were dropped on it.

On some afternoons, we were permitted to leave the ship using one of our landing boats to land on the beach and swim. That was my first experience at swimming in and tasting saltwater. I could hardly wait to get back to the ship to take a freshwater shower because I felt so sticky when the saltwater dried on me.

Letters from home were eagerly awaited. Dad wrote his notes on his prescription pads. His handwriting was typical of a hurried doctor and full of abbreviations. For example, I ultimately came to understand that the letter "c" with a line above it, meant "with" (from the Latin "cum"). Reading his letters usually took most of my spare time for an afternoon, even if they were only three or four sheets long. Letters from Aunts Olga and Jewell were always neatly typed. The most interesting letters came from Jean Anderson, the "girl next door" in Cannon Falls. She kept me informed of the activities of my school friends that I had left behind.

One of my tasks at Bikini was to go over our vessel from bow to stern and note any pre-existing physical damage to any of the electronic equipment and to log the information on a special form. Those notes were to be used for reference after the bomb drop to see what damage the *Artemis* might have suffered from the test blast, even though the drop was going to occur at the horizon some twenty miles away.

Somewhat to my surprise, Mr. Collins came to me one day and said that if I wanted to be on board to witness the bomb drop, I would have to sign up for another four-year hitch. I had no trouble telling him, "No, thanks!" I was ready to go home and persue my college education. In retrospect, it was fortuitous I chose not to stay. In recent years, several television documentaries have shown that the men who witnessed the explosion even from twenty miles away have had an unusually high incidence of leukemia and other forms of cancer due to radiation exposure during that event.

Homeward Bound

A few days after my decision to leave the *Artemis*, I was transferred to the USS *Rockingham*, APA 229, which took me and a few hundred more sailors back to Pearl Harbor. APA was the acronym for Amphibious Passenger Attack. The *Rockingham* was basically a troop ship designed to carry soldiers close to shore where landing craft could be launched to take them into battle. It was another flat bottom boat, similar to the *Artemis*. There were no amenities on the *Rockingham*. We slept in bunks four tiers high. We ate standing up in the mess hall at tables that were four feet off the floor – not exactly leisurely dining. We spent our spare time out on deck reading and commiserating, but all of us aboard had one thing in common. We were going home!

However, we were disappointed to learn that we would have a layover in Pearl Harbor instead of continuing on to San Francisco. Perhaps the ship needed some overhaul and provisioning. After a week or so we were underway again. As I recall, we docked at Treasure Island in California. From there it was a long, but happy train ride to Minneapolis and on to the U.S. Naval Air Station at Wold Chamberlain Field.

Close, but Not Quite There

I arrived at the naval base on July 2nd anticipating I would be home with my family in Cannon Falls in time to celebrate my nineteenth birthday two days later. It was not to be. The staff at the base said they would be taking off early the next day for the holiday so there would not be time to process my discharge until after the Fourth. I was discharged on Friday, July 5, 1946, but as I recall, we still had a great celebration when I arrived in Cannon Falls. It was so good to be home, to think about getting on with my life, and getting on with my life by starting in college on my way to an electrical engineering degree.

Fast Forward

On September 30, 2017, I was pleased to be selected to participate in an Honors Flight Network trip, a program dedicated to honoring veterans for their service to our country. Accompanied by my oldest daughter, Elizabeth, I boarded an airliner completely filled with World War II and Korean War veterans and their accompanying family members. We flew to Washington, D.C. where we were loaded onto three large coach busses. Our entourage enjoyed a police escort throughout the city for a full day of touring the striking war memorials. We witnessed the poignant changing of the guard at the Tomb of the Unknown Soldier at Arlington National Cemetery.

Our group was fairly conspicuous in our brightly colored Honor Flight t-shirts and ID badges on lanyards. While the entire tour was extraordinary, I was surprised how I reacted whenever a stranger approached me to say, "Thank you for your service." Elizabeth asked me why I was uncomfortable with that. I said, "Because frankly, I got more out of the Navy than the Navy got out of me. I got a career out the deal."

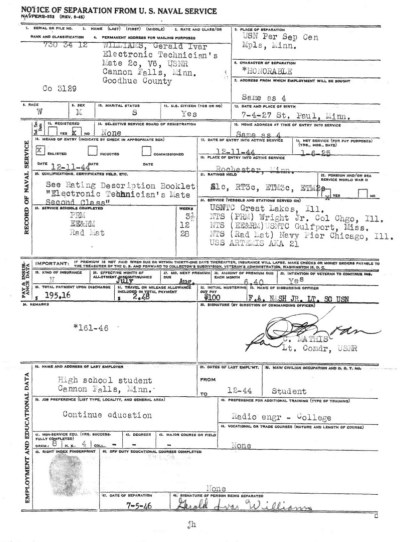

NOTICE OF SEPARATION FROM U. S. NAVAL SERVICE
NAVPERS-553 (REV. 8-45)

1. SERIAL OR FILE NO.	2. NAME (LAST) (FIRST) (MIDDLE)	3. RATE AND CLASS/OR RANK AND CLASSIFICATION 4. PERMANENT ADDRESS FOR MAILING PURPOSES	5. PLACE OF SEPARATION
730 34 12	WILLIAMS, Gerald Ivar	Electronic Technician's Mate 2c, V6, USNR Cannon Falls, Minn. Goodhue County	USN Per Sep Cen Mpls, Minn.

6. CHARACTER OF SEPARATION
*HONORABLE

7. ADDRESS FROM WHICH EMPLOYMENT WILL BE SOUGHT

Co 3129

Same as 4

8. RACE	9. SEX	10. MARITAL STATUS	11. U.S. CITIZEN (YES OR NO)	12. DATE AND PLACE OF BIRTH
W	M	S	Yes	7-4-27 St. Paul, Minn.

13. REGISTERED YES x NO None

14. SELECTIVE SERVICE BOARD OF REGISTRATION

15. HOME ADDRESS AT TIME OF ENTRY INTO SERVICE
Same as 4

RECORD OF NAVAL SERVICE

16. MEANS OF ENTRY (INDICATE BY CHECK IN APPROPRIATE BOX)
[X] ENLISTED [ ] INDUCTED [ ] COMMISSIONED
DATE 12-11-44 DATE DATE

17. DATE OF ENTRY INTO ACTIVE SERVICE
12-11-44

18. NET SERVICE (FOR PAY PURPOSES) (YRS., MOS., DAYS)
1-6-25

19. PLACE OF ENTRY INTO ACTIVE SERVICE
Rochester, Minn.

20. QUALIFICATIONS, CERTIFICATES HELD, ETC.
See Rating Description Booklet "Electronic Technician's Mate Second Class"

21. RATINGS HELD
Slc, RT3c, ETM3c, ETM2c

22. FOREIGN AND/OR SEA SERVICE WORLD WAR II [x] YES [ ] NO

23. SERVICE SCHOOLS COMPLETED	WEEKS
PRM	3½
EE&RM	12
Rad Mat	28

24. SERVICE (VESSELS AND STATIONS SERVED ON)
USNTC Great Lakes, Ill.
NTS (PRM) Wright Jr. Col Chgo, Ill.
NTS (EE&RM) USNTC Gulfport, Miss.
NTS (Rad Mat) Navy Pier Chicago, Ill.
USS ARTEMIS AKA 21

PAY & INSURANCE DATA

IMPORTANT: IF PREMIUM IS NOT PAID WHEN DUE OR WITHIN THIRTY-ONE DAYS THEREAFTER, INSURANCE WILL LAPSE. MAKE CHECKS OR MONEY ORDERS PAYABLE TO THE TREASURER OF THE U. S. AND FORWARD TO COLLECTOR'S SUBDIVISION, VETERAN'S ADMINISTRATION, WASHINGTON 25, D. C.

25. KIND OF INSURANCE	26. EFFECTIVE MONTH OF ALLOTMENT DISCONTINUANCE	27. MO. NEXT PREMIUM DUE	28. AMOUNT OF PREMIUM EACH MONTH	29. INTENTION OF VETERAN TO CONTINUE INS.
N	July	Aug.	6.40	Yes

30. TOTAL PAYMENT UPON DISCHARGE	31. TRAVEL OR MILEAGE ALLOWANCE INCLUDED IN TOTAL PAYMENT	32. INITIAL MUSTERING OUT PAY	33. NAME OF DISBURSING OFFICER
195.16	2.48	$100	F.A. NASH JR. LT. SC USN

34. REMARKS

*161-46

33. SIGNATURE (BY DIRECTION OF COMMANDING OFFICER)
C. MATHIS
Lt. Comdr, USNR

EMPLOYMENT AND EDUCATIONAL DATA

35. NAME AND ADDRESS OF LAST EMPLOYER	37. DATES OF LAST EMPL'MT.	38. MAIN CIVILIAN OCCUPATION AND D. O. T. NO.
High school student Cannon Falls, Minn.	FROM TO 12-44	Student

39. JOB PREFERENCE (LIST TYPE, LOCALITY, AND GENERAL AREA)
Continue education

40. PREFERENCE FOR ADDITIONAL TRAINING (TYPE OF TRAINING)
Radio engr - College

41. NON-SERVICE EDU. (YRS. SUCCESSFULLY COMPLETED)
GRAM. 8 H. S. 4 COLL. —

42. DEGREES — 43. MAJOR COURSE OR FIELD —

44. VOCATIONAL OR TRADE COURSES (NATURE AND LENGTH OF COURSE)
None

45. RIGHT INDEX FINGERPRINT

46. OFF DUTY EDUCATIONAL COURSES COMPLETED
None

47. DATE OF SEPARATION
7-5-46

48. SIGNATURE OF PERSON BEING SEPARATED
Gerald Ivar Williams

jh

This document erroneously says I entered the Navy in Rochester, Minnesota, instead of Minneapolis.

Chapter 5

MY COLLEGE YEARS
July 1946 to December 1950

Where shall I go?

The time I spent in the Navy studying state-of-the-art electronic equipment solidified my desire to become an electrical engineer. As a veteran, I was qualified to receive my education under the GI Bill of Rights. Once enrolled in a college, the government would pay for my tuition and books and I would receive a monthly stipend of $75 to live on. Up to that point, the only college I had considered was the Institute of Technology at the University of Minnesota, but the classes I wanted were full.

I've already explained how my stepmother Viola helped me enroll at St. Olaf College and find a place to live with Mrs. Winger, who turned out to be somewhat the motherly type. I felt accountable for my time in her home, particularly when I used her phone. My roommate, Russell Beck, and I had very little in common except for sharing a room and the double bed. We both usually went home on the weekends, so there was not much opportunity for us to socialize together.

I was still in need of a means of transportation. Detroit had not fully recovered from its conversion to building weapons of war, so buying a new car was out of the question. They were just not available yet. But my father, anticipating my need for a car upon my return from the Navy, knew of a Model A Ford coupe owned by the father of our milkman. The old gentleman was no longer able to drive. He had purchased the car in 1929 and only used it to drive a few miles back and forth from his son's farm to town for morning coffee with his buddies. The car was gloss black with yellow wheels and looked really sharp. As I recall, it had less than 20,000 miles on it, and it even had the original tires. The money to buy it came from the war bonds I had sent home every payday while in the Navy. My recollection is that the car cost about $600. I found the original sales brochure in the door pocket.

Jerry and his Model A

Over the next four years, I put a lot of time and effort into that car to meet my needs. It had no heater, so I fabricated a piece of sheet metal around the exhaust manifold to carry some of the engine heat into the car. I could shut it on or off with a little grille from a war surplus radio. It helped some, but not much on the really cold winter days. I added turn signals and sealed beam headlights. They made driving a bit safer. I put a used car radio on the shelf behind my head. Putting the radio under the dashboard was out of the question because that is where the gas tank is in the Model A. Gasoline was gravity-fed from that tank directly into the carburetor. It was a simple car. I later passed it on to my brother, Keith, who drove it to New Haven, Connecticut, where he went to school and he sold it there.

Jobs During My College Years

I was not really enthused about attending St. Olaf College, because I thought I would not be able to get started with the kind of courses required for a Bachelor of Electrical Engineering degree. However, I was excited about the possibility of getting a job at the college radio station, WCAL. I saw the radio station as opportunity to apply and extend my knowledge of radio technology. I inquired about working there as a student and was directed to Mr. Milford Jensen, the station manager. Mr. Jensen offered me a job as an engineer, on the condition that I obtain the requisite FCC First Class License required to operate WCAL's 5000-watt transmitter.

Acting on Mr. Jensen's direction, I drove to the FCC office in St Paul. With all the training I had in the Navy, I breezed through the eight-hour written exam. My license arrived in the mail a few weeks later.

I committed nearly all of my spare time to the radio station. Mr. Jensen seemed to have a never-ending amount of work for me, for which I was paid forty-five cents an hour. Working at WCAL was welcome compensation for not being able to enroll at the University of Minnesota immediately after my discharge from the Navy.

"Jens," as we affectionately called him, was a pioneer in radio broadcasting and one of the founders of the radio station. He was an excellent tutor and was one of the men who strongly influenced my life. He taught me the importance of attention to detail and he was patient and willing to let me learn from my mistakes.

At WCAL I learned how to stretch a dollar. WCAL was a non-commercial radio station operating on a limited budget, yet it justifiably prided itself on the quality of its programming and its broadcast signal.

Working to Earn Money

I earned a little extra spending money that first year at St. Olaf by renting out a portable sound system that I had built and by repairing radios and installing TV antennas and receivers on the weekends in Cannon Falls. Because I could use the money, I occasionally did some weekend transmitter relief work at KDHL radio station in Faribault, fifteen miles south of Northfield.

Jens did not own a car. He lived in an area known as Walden Place, adjacent to the St. Olaf campus and he simply walked the few hundred yards to work. I believe his radio at home was perpetually tuned to WCAL because we received a phone call anytime he heard something he didn't think was right. He was usually gracious and constructive with his criticism.

One homecoming weekend we had WCAL as sparking clean and orderly as it could possibly be. I was operating the transmitter when a very tall, distinguished-looking gentleman, whom I had never seen, walked right into the transmitter room and started nosing around. As politely as I could I said, "I'm sorry sir, but the station rules do not allow visitors in this area." He said, "Son, I built this transmitter." I quickly responded, "You must be Dr. Skifter." I don't recall the rest of the conversation, but I imagine that he was pleased to be recognized. I considered it a great privilege to meet him. Later in 1998, WCAL gave me a complimentary copy of Hector Skifter's autobiography.

After graduating from St. Olaf in 1922, Hector Skifter went on to become a nationally recognized radio engineer. For several years he was the chief engineer at Western Radio Engineering, a business formed by the Hubbard family who owned KSTP, St. Paul's prominent radio station.

It was during that era that Dr. Skifter designed and built the transmitter for WCAL. Jens told me the WCAL transmitter was the prototype Final Stage Driver for KSTP's 50,000-watt transmit-

Monitoring a program, veteran Gerald Williams of Cannon Falls, Minn., operates a speech input unit.

ter. In later years, Skifter established Airborne Instruments Laboratories on Long Island, New York.

During the summer following my first year at St. Olaf, the WCAL Board of Directors allocated the money to replace the Skifter AM transmitter since it was at least twenty years old. I lived and worked at the radio station that summer, sleeping on a cot in the back-up emergency generator room. Installing the new transmitter necessitated that we make field strength measurements of the broadcast signal to prove that the new transmitter was operating within the FCC authorized power limit. Since Jens did not have a car, we used my Model A Ford to drive all over the back roads of Rice County taking those measurements. That trip gave me a good opportunity to know Jens better. The field strength meter we used to make those measurements had been designed and built by Hector Skifter some years before.

My Favorite Professors

My professors at St. Olaf were interesting individuals whom I failed to appreciate until two years later while at the University where most of my instructors were only paid TA's (teaching assistants) working on their graduate degrees.

My physics lab professor at St. Olaf was Dr. Erik Hetle, an elderly gentleman of Norwegian ancestry. On one occasion when we were performing experiments with weights, string, and pulleys, one of the students asked Dr. Hetle for a scissors to cut the string to length. Mr. Hetle told him to use his pocketknife. The student sheepishly replied that he didn't have a pocketknife. Whereupon we were given a "time-out lecture" about the necessity of owning a pocketknife if we were ever to make a valid claim to manhood. That afternoon there was a run on pocket-knives at the Northfield hardware stores.

Another of my colorful professors was my English teacher, Hjalmar Lokensgaard. He "coerced" me to write, something I disliked doing in high school because, as a perfectionist, my papers were a mess from all the erasures. (I enjoy writing now because the computer provides delete/copy/insert and spell-check commands. I don't need to use a rubber eraser anymore.)

I also came to appreciate Dr. Harold Dittmanson, my religion professor. He coached me through some awkward personal problems and I even did some baby-sitting for his family.

The activity that was to become the most significant factor in my life – although I did not realize it at the time – was the St. Olaf Band. Dr. Donald Berglund was the director. There were more alto saxophone players wanting than were needed so we had to come in for try-outs. I did not do well because I had not played my instrument since the last summer band concert in Cannon Falls in 1943 before I went into the Navy. But because the band needed a baritone saxophone and the college owned one, Dr. Berglund said I could play in the band if I switched to that instrument.

In that position in the band, I was seated next to a young blond lady to my left who played alto sax. She introduced herself as Shirley Hetland from Valley City, North Dakota. Shirley and I were destined to become good friends for most of our lives.

To my right was another young lady who had been switched from B-flat clarinet to alto clarinet. Her name was Lorraine

Hoffman from St. James, Minnesota. She had a twin sister named Florraine seated at her right who had been switched from clarinet to the school's bassoon. Because the twins were inseparable, the three of us soon became good friends.

At that time, I was having a lot of difficulty understanding chemistry, largely because I signed up for a chemistry class that was intended for students who had studied chemistry in high school. The St. Olaf professor, Dr. Paul Glasoe, assumed that we already knew the basics. The truth was I had only three months of chemistry in high school before I enlisted in the Navy, so I was way behind the other students before I even got started. I should have signed up for the freshman class for students without any previous chemistry background. I would have gotten the same credit, but I did not realize that at the time.

During a break in a band rehearsal, I mentioned my chemistry problem to Lorraine. She kindly offered to help me since she

Williams Family, 1949, Viola, Jerry, Roger, Marilyn, Marland, Keith

had taken that class two years before. Our biggest problem was finding a location to meet for tutoring. We both lived off-campus in private homes and neither house was suitable for studying together. We tried to work in the library, but we were frequently reprimanded by the librarians for talking. We changed our plan to have supper together in the cafeteria and then find a quiet space for her to help me. After a few weeks of her help I managed to get a passing grade in chemistry, and I began to look at Lorraine differently.

Surprised by Jesus

Because of working at the radio station, my classwork at St. Olaf didn't get as much attention as it should have. In retrospect, I suspect that's why, even under the watchful eye of my religion professor, I still hadn't met Jesus Christ face to face. Later in life, I came to realize that part of God's plan for my life included the wife He had in mind for me.

Perhaps you, like me as a boy, wondered who your spouse would be and what that person was doing at the same instant. I never realized that God would or even cared to play a hand in the selection of a spouse. I thought fate had more to do with it than anything else. I believe now that fate is the name for what happens when we don't let Him have control of our lives to carry out His plan.

I'd like to digress here to wonder if when a child loses a committed Christian parent, in my case my birth mother and later on my stepmother, if God allows those saints to continue overseeing their children's lives. I don't know of any theological basis for it, but I have had so many experiences where I felt the intervention and leading of an unseen spirit in my life, that I am convinced someone with a special interest kept me from harm and showed me the right course of action. One reason I wonder about this is because I had not yet begun to use the power of prayer at that time, nor had I committed my life to Jesus. Despite that, the right things seemed to happen to me.

Perhaps my mother and/or my stepmother are my special guardian angels, or they intercede for me with the angels. Perhaps their intercession could even extend to the selection of a wife for me. After all, what mother isn't concerned about the woman that her son will choose as a wife, and what better place to oversee this selection process than from heaven. I don't have any theological basis for my feeling, but someday I will have the opportunity to check it out first-hand.

Back to my story. Lorraine had to compete for my spare time on very unequal terms with the radio station. One afternoon she came over to the radio station and asked me to take her to a spiritual emphasis meeting where Reverend Reuben Gornitzka would be speaking. He was the senior pastor at Central Lutheran Church in downtown Minneapolis. I was less than enthusiastic about her request, but I somehow felt compelled to attend.

Reverend Gornitzka made a statement that night that caught me off balance, but when he repeated it, it made a lot of sense. He was talking about Jesus Christ and he said, "Jesus either had to be the Son of God, as He said he was, or else He was the greatest faker that ever lived. There can be no middle ground." With His life He accomplished something that none of the world's greatest political leaders have ever achieved. He divided our calendar into a before and after without the use of either a pen or a sword.

C. S. Lewis, the famous British writer who became a Christian about as late in life as I did, said it a little differently. He said some people are willing to call Jesus a great moral teacher, but how can you call a man a great moral teacher who claims to be the Son of God? If He wasn't who He claimed to be, then He would have to be classed as a lunatic, or the greatest faker who ever lived. and who could accept a lunatic as a great moral teacher? (C.S. Lewis, *Mere Christianity*, 1952) You can't have it both ways and neither could I that night.

As I walked Lorraine back to her rooming house that night, I kept mulling over Reverend Gornitzka's comments. It must have been a dull evening for Lorraine because after we were married, I was able to skim through her diary and there was no mention of that night, which for me was one of the real turning points in my life.

At that point my friendship with Lorraine began to gradually develop into something more serious. We spent many hours just sitting and talking, much of it in my Model A Ford at the Carleton College Arboretum where we could be alone together. We discovered that we had many ideas in common. We had similar values, hopes, and dreams. I think that we both thought that we had something special in each other, yet I couldn't come to the point of making a commitment to her.

Lorraine and Florraine spent the next summer working as

66

waitresses at Birchmont Lodge near Bemidji. I stayed at St. Olaf to work at WCAL. I decided to stay at St. Olaf for my sophomore year because I had come to love the school and the faculty, but most of all Lorraine. I also realized I could take courses that would apply to my engineering career without sacrificing much from my future classes at the University.

For that second year I lived in the walk-out basement of a house at 105 South Orchard Street in Northfield with my brother, Keith, and two pre-med students, Alvin Waters, also from Cannon Falls, and Harry Munson, a free-spirited student from Norway. The Wilson family lived upstairs, but we had almost no interaction with them. Downstairs, we had one large room with a kitchenette, so we prepared a lot of our own meals. It seemed as though I was appointed to be the chief cook. My meals were very simple for Keith and me, mostly coming out of cans.

The University

In the fall of 1948, I transferred to the University of Minnesota and enrolled as an electrical engineering major at the Institute of Technology. Studying at the U of M was quite a different experience from student life at St. Olaf College.

I found a rooming house within walking distance of my classes on 4th Street Southeast in Minneapolis. It was in an area known as Dinkytown with a few stores, a barber shop, and a Snyder's Drug store that also served food. I ate a lot of my meals there as well as bedtime snacks with my three housemates. One was studying aeronautical engineering, one was a law student, and the third was majoring in accounting. Almost nightly after supper we played cards, usually canasta, for an hour or so and then we walked to Snyders for ice cream.

There were no girl students in any of my classes, so after a few weeks, I started wondering what Lorraine was doing after her graduation. I really missed her companionship and wondered if I had made a mistake in breaking off our relationship. Lorraine suddenly became more important. I'll tell you about this in the next chapter, but first a little more about finishing my college education.

By taking all twelve quarters in continuous succession – no summer vacations, I was able to graduate from the University on December 21, 1950, off-peak of the normal graduation cycle. The job market was very slim at that time for electrical engineers, particularly in Minnesota, but I was one of the lucky ones. I received two job offers, one from RCA, the other from Zenith Radio.

College graduate, 1950

Working While at The University of Minnesota, 1948-1950, age 23

In December of 1950, I was completing my education in electrical engineering at the University of Minnesota. I contemplated where I could get the kind of job I would need now that Lorraine and I were married. I talked to several people who might have contacts for me. There were simply no job openings at that time in the Twin Cities area for electrical engineers in my sphere of interest. In fact, in 1950 there were very few electronics manufacturers in Minnesota, not like it is now in the 2000s.

Since I had been servicing radios and television receivers as a means of support while I was in school, I became familiar with one small local radio manufacturer, the Setchel Carlson Company in New Brighton. I wrote a letter and visited them, but there were no openings.

In Cannon Falls, my father knew Ed Miller, the manager of the local telephone company. Ed told me the Minnesota Telephone Company which owned the Cannon Falls exchange might have something for me. Ed and I spent most of one day traveling in Southeastern Minnesota visiting their installations, but that turned out to be another dead end. There would be no design engineering in their jobs, only equipment maintenance.

George Kaisersatt, a trooper with the Minnesota Highway Patrol stationed in Zumbrota, offered to get me an interview with their office in St. Paul, but it would be as a serviceman for squad-car radios. I was not interested in that either.

Chapter 6

MY TWO WIVES – THE HOFFMAN TWINS

Identical twin girls were born to Christian and Emmy Hoffman on December 29, 1926, in the St. James, Minnesota, hospital. They gave them rhyming names: Lorraine Laura and Florraine Flora. The baby girls were quite the Christmas gift for this couple because they had not married until Emmy was nearly 29 years old and Chris was already 36. Chris and Emmy's parents were Germans who immigrated to America in the 1880s seeking a better

The Hoffman family. front: Chris, Waldo, Emmy, back: Lorraine, Florraine.

opportunity for themselves and their future families.

The twins were exceptionally identical in appearance and they always dressed alike. Their classmates could only tell them apart when they spoke, because their voices were slightly different. They were inseparable until they each married.

When they reached elementary school age, the girls' destinies were impacted by a visit from their Wisconsin Lutheran Synod pastor. He confronted their mother Emmy about why she had not enrolled her girls in the congregation's parochial school. She told the pastor she believed they would get a better education in the St. James public school. The pastor was so upset by her answer that he became quite nasty. His behavior was all that Emmy needed to remove the girls from the church's Sunday School and immediately enrolled them in the Sunday School of the (Norwegian) First Lutheran Church of St. James. That ELC congregation was affiliated with St. Olaf College in Northfield so when Emmy and Chris considered a college education for their daughters, St. Olaf was a natural choice.

Lorraine and Florraine were confirmed in the Lutheran faith at First Lutheran Church by Reverend Harald Strand on March 29, 1942. They graduated from St. James High School in 1944, and were the first young women in their extended family to attend college. Some of the elder relatives felt a

Lorraine and Florraine

college education would be a total waste of time and money for women destined to only be mothers and housewives. Fortunately, Chris and Emmy had greater aspirations for their daughters. Chris was a bright man and always regretted having to leave school to work on the farm after his 8th grade year. Both he and Emmy valued education.

As you now know, when I enrolled at St. Olaf I was seated

next to Lorraine and Florraine in the band. After a few months I found myself in love with Lorraine, so instead of transferring to the "U" for my sophomore year as planned, I decided to stay at St. Olaf one more year. However, I broke up with Lorraine after just a few weeks because the relationship was moving too fast for me.

After I transferred to the "U" for my junior year, I realized I had made a mistake in breaking up with her. By then Lorraine had graduated. With no idea where she might be, I took a chance and wrote her a letter in care of her parents' address. Within a week she responded, which told me a spark of love was still there. She was teaching home economics at the high school in Truman, Minnesota, about 20 miles southeast of St. James.

We were engaged three months later but had to delay marriage for a year because she had to fulfill her teaching contract. My 1929 Model A Ford coupe (with no heater) carried me many times to Truman to pick up Lorraine for a weekend visit to St. James. On Sunday night we drove back to Truman and then I headed north to Minneapolis. Usually I got so sleepy on the drive north that I stopped in Mankato at a popcorn wagon for a large bag of popcorn. Those salty kernels kept me busy chewing and then made me so thirsty that I couldn't fall asleep.

Occasionally Lorraine took the bus to Minneapolis on Friday after school. I would pick her up at the station and we'd drive to Cannon Falls for the weekend. Meanwhile her twin, Florraine, was teaching home ec in Heron Lake, Minnesota, about 35 miles southwest of St. James. Florraine was engaged to Joe Wangen, whom she met riding a bus back to Heron Lake.

Bruce	Waldo	Joseph	Florraine	Lorraine	Gerald	Keith	John
Govig '48	Hoffman '55	Wangen '47	Hoffman '48	Hoffman '48	Williams '50	Williams '51	Strom

| Barbara | Vicki | | June 11th, 1950 | | | Marilyn | Margaret |
| Strand '51 | Norstog '48 | | First Lutheran Church, St. James, MN | | | Williams '52 | Milang '48 |

Their mother said they could finance only one wedding that year, so the girls would have to decide whose it would be. The twins decided on a double wedding. It was the talk of the town. We were married on June 11, 1950, in First Lutheran Church. The father of Florraine's groom was a pastor so he and Pastor Harald Strand shared the nuptial "stage." Among the bridesmaids and groomsmen there were eleven "Oles" from St. Olaf College and one "Auggie" from Augsburg College in Minneapolis.

Lorraine and I had fifty-six wonderful years together that brought us three life-enriching children, five grandchildren, and now eleven great-grandchildren. Unfortunately, Lorraine developed severe rheumatoid arthritis not long after our third child, Paul, was born. She was only in her early thirties. Her joint pain was controlled with prednisone for about 35 years. What we didn't know was that the prednisone was slowly weakening her bones. Lorraine began experiencing fractures from osteoporosis followed by surgeries for her damaged joints – at least one each year starting from age 52. For the last six years of her life Lorraine was bed-ridden with unhealed fractures in her back and right arm. Not even the great doctors at the Mayo Clinic could help her.

Jerry and Lorraine

Shortly before she died on May 12, 2006, Lorraine asked me to promise to look after Florraine after the anticipated death of Florraine's second husband, William "Bill" Trygstad. I assured her I would do that, but asked, "What would you think if I married Florraine, because that would be the easiest way to care for her?" She replied, "That would be all right."

A year after Lorraine died, I decided I had to leave the retirement home on Lake Hubert that we built together in 1987. I simply could not stay in that house alone any longer. I had no neighbors in the winter. I didn't know where I would move to, but at a Christmas party that year at Florraine's daughter, Jody's home I told my adult children they had to retrieve any of their poossessions from the Lake Hubert house because I was putting

74

it up for sale. They immediately wanted to know where I was planning to move to. I said I didn't know yet, but I knew I didn't want to move back to the Twin Cities.

Florraine suggested Northfield. Bingo! Northfield was much closer to my children and grandchildren, my sister, and Florraine. Northfield is the home of St Olaf College with all those happy memories, and it's close to Cannon Falls, where I grew up. It was the perfect decision. The house I bought in Northfield at 1107 Cannon Valley Drive in 2007 was not yet finished inside. Lorraine had been so talented at decorating but now I felt incapable of making all those decisions: carpet, paint colors, wallpaper, lighting, plumbing fixtures, appliances, etc. My oldest daughter, Elizabeth, and Florraine came to my rescue and had a good time making those selections.

Florraine's second husband, Bill, died in January 2009. In keeping with my promise to Lorraine, I stepped in to help Florraine and her daughter Jody with all the arrangements they faced in settling Bill's estate and to make certain that Florraine was financially secure.

After we had things in good order, marrying each other seemed to be a natural next step for both of us. Our children were comfortable with the idea because neither of us was bringing a stranger into our established families. We were married on June 6, 2009, at Bethel Lutheran Church in Northfield. Then we faced the challenge of merging our two households with the accumulations of our lifetimes into one home.

Loneliness is a terrible thing when you live alone. Our new life together was the right choice. In a sense, Florraine and I were both "leftovers," but leftovers can be pretty tasty after they get warmed up. We believed that ours was a match made in heaven begun 63 years earlier in the St. Olaf band room.

Chapter 7

THE FIRST YEARS OF OUR RICHLY BLESSED MARRIAGE 1950-1957

Our Honeymoon

After our unique double wedding ceremony in St. James, Lorraine and I headed for Red Wing where I had arranged with my father to use his forty-foot cabin cruiser for a few days. It was kept on the Mississippi River on the north side of Red Wing, floating and tethered in a large wooden structure with other cruisers.

Jerry & Lorraine leaving for their honeymoon

We had to make a stopover in Cannon Falls to pick up a small outboard motor and a can of fuel for the eight-foot dinghy. Dad did not want us to take the cruiser out without the usual crew because he felt I could not handle it alone, but the dinghy would afford us the opportunity to motor down to Lake Pepin for a swim and a visit to our family's cottage at Wacouta where I had worked many hours and updated the wiring.

Our first night on the cruiser was sweet and restful with pleasant memories of our wedding day still fresh in our minds.

For the second night, we decided to go into town for a nice dinner at Nybo's Restaurant and see a movie. If Lorraine was still here, she could probably name the film we saw. When we emerged from the theater, it was raining so hard the water was running over the sidewalk curbs.

After waiting a long time for the rain to let up, Lorraine suggested we take off our "good" clothes and make a run for it. We pared down to a bare minimum and took off running. Fortunately, no one was around to see us, but the next day a gathering of boat owners enjoying their morning coffee smiled at the pile of clothes I carried back to the boat. They gave me that all-knowing look because my father had told them we would be using the boat for our honeymoon.

Honeymoon cruiser

We got dressed and went into town for breakfast or lunch and decided this was a perfect day for a boat ride. I was able to get the dinghy off the cruiser and into the water and installed the outboard motor with much-appreciated support from Lorraine. I think Lorraine wore only her swimsuit and a top and I had on my swim shorts. It was a comfortable sunny day, and the first several miles on the river went smoothly until we reached the place where the river splits into two channels. The motor suddenly quit, and I was unable to re-start it.

I surmised a slug of old oil might have plugged the carburetor and caused the motor to quit. I knew how to fix it, but it would be difficult at that spot in the river. On top of that, we were drifting quickly toward the channel that would take us to Wisconsin, not to Lake Pepin where we could get help.

I asked Lorraine to use one of the two oars we had onboard to steer the boat into the channel toward Lake Pepin. After a valiant attempt on her part I realized she did not have the physical strength needed, so we traded places and I took over by rowing as best I could to get us into the Pepin channel. I failed at that but I was able to get us into a calm part of the river so I could lift the motor into the boat.

My guardian angel must have been with us that day because I glanced around and spotted a tool kit. After removing the carburetor and a bit of disassembly, I saw my hunch was correct. I needed gasoline to wash out the oil plug. I don't remember how I removed that plug, but once again my angel must have coached me that day.

I reassembled everything and re-mounted the motor. A few

quick pulls on the starter rope had the motor purring and we were on our way back to Red Wing. We did not have time at that point for a swim or to go to Wacouta, but Lorraine was elated thatwe had survived that experience.

With so much time sitting while I was fixing the motor, Lorraine got a terrible sunburn. It took several days for it to clear up and also required lengthy recitations later to explain how it happened.

We gathered up our belongings from the cruiser and drove to Cannon Falls where we were graciously received at my father's home for supper and invited to stay the night. It was not our anticipated honeymoon so we made up for it later with a more traditional honeymoon trip to Niagara Falls that autumn.

Our First Temporary Abode, June-August 1950

The next day, after saying goodbye to my father and his third wife, Phyllis, we drove to our first temporary abode at 2267 Carter Avenue in St. Paul. We could not move into the University Housing Project yet because the trailer we reserved was still occupied, so we arranged to sublet an apartment for the summer from Wendell & Jeanne Frerichs, who we knew from our St. Olaf days. At that time, Wendell was a student at Luther Seminary which was within walking distance from this apartment on Carter Avenue.

We carried our belongings (mostly clothing) from the car up to our little second-floor apartment, happy to have a place to begin married life. After settling in, we discovered we needed to buy some things to start "keeping house" – things we took for granted in our parents' homes, like a toaster, ironing board, cooling fan, etc. It was fun doing that kind of shopping together for the first time. I think we shopped at Montgomery Ward's on University Avenue. I still use that ironing board after a bit of re-welding.

Our Second Temporary Abode, August-December 1950

When the summer ended, we vacated the Frerichs' apartment and took possession of the trailer house I had reserved in the University Village at 29th Street and Como Avenue. Our neighbors were several hundred trailer dwellers. From there I caught a streetcar to the university campus in Minneapolis. Lorraine was happy to discover there were several wives living there whom she knew from St. James and St. Olaf College. She also had the use of our car so she was able to go for groceries and supplies. She could do our laundry in the machines within walking distance of our trailer and prepare supper on a stove in the trailer.

Trailer home at University Village

I expected to graduate in three months, so it didn't seem logical for her to look for a job. On the weekends we usually drove to Cannon Falls or St. James, or both, to visit our parents and siblings.

I enrolled in another summer quarter of electrical engineering classes. After breakfast I took the streetcar to the University and returned home about 3:00 in the afternoon. The summer classes were my favorites because we concentrated on just two subjects and I got my best grades in those classes. They also enabled me to complete the curriculum sooner so I could graduate in December of 1951 at age 24.

My First Job and Eight Months in Chicago

As my class approached graduation there were no posted job openings for electrical engineers in Minnesota, so I was pleased to see two scheduled interviews posted on the bulletin board. One was with RCA, the other with Zenith Radio. They looked like surprise gifts intended just for me since those jobs were exactly what I was interested in doing.

The RCA job would have required moving to Camden, New Jersey, and it offered a salary of $265 a month. The RCA job involved designing radio and television receivers. The Zenith job required moving to Chicago. Zenith offered a salary of $290 a month and involved developing color television receivers before they were being manufactured.

Another factor entered into the choice I made. You may recall I earned money on the weekends servicing radios and TVs while in high school and college. That experience gave me the impression that Zenith built a better product than RCA and I wanted to find out how and why.

Making the choice between these two offers was easy on three counts: 1) Chicago was much closer to Minnesota, 2) Zenith offered more money, and 3) color TV was just in its infancy so the work would be more interesting and could last quite a long time.

After the Christmas and New Year's celebrations were over, Lorraine and I loaded up the blue 1947 Chevrolet coupe my Dad gave us as a wedding gift. That Chevy had been my stepmother Viola's car, but sadly, she died nine months before our wedding, so it was available. I missed Viola at our wedding, but she had already approved of Lorraine so that was a bit of consolation for me.

When we arrived in Chicago in January of 1951, I drove directly to Zenith to find John Rennick who had interviewed me at the "U." He introduced me to his boss, Jesse Brown, Zenith's chief engineer. Mr. Brown was the person that signed my job offer. They asked if we had found a place to live yet. My answer was in the negative, so they told me to return to start work after we found housing.

I cannot recall how we did that search, but we found a flat at 2047 North 73rd Avenue in Elmwood Park. It was half of an upper floor in an apartment building about a mile from the Zenith factory. It was in a very good location because my new boss, John Rennick, lived only two blocks away. He and I took turns driving to Zenith each day so our wives could use the family cars for shopping and errands. It also meant Lorraine immediately had a friend to advise her where to shop and how to get there. We soon became good friends with the Rennicks and were invited to their home for meals and Lorraine reciprocated in kind. That summer was very hot. Lorraine also looked after me by having a bath drawn so when I got home from Zenith I could cool down. We spent many weekends outdoors in the parks to stay cool.

Instead of jumping right into the design routine at Zenith, I was put through a sort of training program – a very valuable experience. I was assigned to the Component Analysis Lab for three months. The knowledge I gained working there has served me well in all of my engineering projects ever since and I learned why Zenith products were so reliable. My job was evaluating vender-supplied samples for conformance to Zenith's specifications and comparing the samples with the similar components already in use. The Zenith slogan was, "The quality goes in before the name goes on."

Apparently, I was a keeper. My next assignment was in the Failure Analysis Lab. Again, I learned more about why Zenith products were so reliable. For my first project, I was sent to the production line to take a new receiver off the assembly line before it was put into a cabinet and bring it back to the lab. I removed all of the vacuum tubes, marked them with an identifier, tested them on a tube tester, and logged the result. I put them back in the chassis, and then connected the TV to an adjustable A/C power source set to 130 volts instead of the usual 120. The set was operated continuously for a period of perhaps six weeks and then was checked for picture abnormalities.

Those test receivers were sold to employees with cabinets at a reduced price. I bought one without the cabinet and made an enclosure from a cardboard box. After we were living in a house, I made a nice wooden cabinet and we used it until color TV broadcasting began.

I had been receiving an electrical engineering society magazine and noticed an ad from a company in St. Paul looking for electrical engineers. By coincidence, Paul and Shirley (Hetland) Tollefson, friends we had double-dated with at St. Olaf, stopped by our apartment to tell us they were on their way to Minnesota to see if Paul could find a job up there because they were unhappy living in Marion, Indiana. I gave Paul the magazine with the job opportunity ad so he could check it out. A few days later on their return trip from Minnesota, they stopped to tell us Paul was hired by that company, Engineering Research Associates, ERA for short. Paul's success in finding a job in Minnesota was all I needed to tell Lorraine I was ready to move, too. She packed the car the next Friday and we took off.

When we arrived at ERA in St. Paul, I was offered an engineering job on the same project to which Paul had been assigned. I accepted. Now, we needed to find a place to live. Paul and Shirley found an apartment at Rose Vista Court in St. Paul near Lexington and Larpenteur streets. Shirley offered to inquire about vacancies. It worked out that we would soon be their neighbors at 1230 Rose Vista Court.

My next task was to quit my job at Zenith in Chicago. My boss was very disappointed with my decision but he kindly understood my reason for leaving.

85

ERA offered to pay for our move to Minnesota, so we hired a packing and moving company. On August 12, 1951, we were once again residents of Minnesota and re-connected with Paul and Shirley who lived just across the street.

After eight months in Illinois, we were very happy now to be back closer to our families. In retrospect it was a very good move, because ERA became one of the pioneers in the computer industry. I worked in that industry for twenty-eight years until I founded Williams Sound Corp. More about that in a later chapter.

Our daughter Elizabeth was delivered by my father at St. John's Hospital in Red Wing on April 19, 1952. During our time at Rose Vista Court, we were visited by Pastor Vernon E. Ander-

Jerry, Lorraine, and Elizabeth at Rose Vista Court, 1952

son who had been selected by the Evangelical Lutheran Church in America (ELCA) to organize a new congregation in our rapidly growing neighborhood of St. Paul. Elizabeth was baptized on May 11, 1952, by Pastor Anderson in the home of my father's sisters and brother: Olga, Jewell, and Stanley Williams. Her sponsors were Lorraine's sister, Florraine, and my brother, Keith. Both sets of grandparents were in attendance.

Several Rose Vista neighbors bought newly built houses in Roseville just a few miles north. Since we were now a family of three, we looked at those houses and decided one of their floor plans would work for us. We selected a house under construction at 2782 Dellwood Avenue, but we needed more money than we had, so we drove to St. James to see if Lorraine's parents could help us. Not only were they willing to help, they were pleased that we had come to them and charged us a very modest rate of interest. We repaid that loan with interest in just a few years. I never forgot their generosity and was pleased to extend loans to our kids when they were purchasing their first homes.

St. Timothy Lutheran Church, St. Paul, 1952-1958

Lorraine and I were greatly impressed by Vern Anderson's enthusiasm, so we attended his worship service the next Sunday after his visit. The congregation met in a modest wooden structure built adjacent to another building that was destined to become the worship center. We met many nice young couples and immediately felt comfortable there, so we returned regularly. St. Timothy Lutheran Church was a great first congregation to begin our married life together and that experience showed us we needed a church to be the center of our married life.

Lorraine and three other ladies decided to form a monthly supper group. We rotated homes for supper. All four ladies were great cooks. At the start, they developed a menu for the next meal and each family provided one course: vegetable, starch, meat, or dessert. After a year or so, the wives agreed it would be simpler for the host family to provide the entire meal. "The Potluck Group" also did activities together as families such as skiing, weekends at a lake cabin, etc., so our kids became friends, too. As I write this, I am the sole survivor out of the four couples, so I have attended each of the seven funerals. It was sad to see those dear friends go.

As I write these stories, it has become apparent how much our family life and friendships revolved around our church. Whenever we moved, we carried those friendships with us so our Christmas card list kept growing until one-by-one those dear friends departed, but we will be re-united one-by-one in heaven.

Lorraine and I both found Pastor Vern's sermons very meaningful, and we were also impressed with how he welcomed and introduced to the congregation each new person to the congregation by name with a little description about them.

Vern was a pastor you could not say no to when he asked you to do something. The first task he asked me to do was to chair the Men's Brotherhood, a group of doctors, lawyers, bankers, teachers, and business owners. My initial reaction was to refuse because I did not feel that I was in their social class. When I mentioned Vern's request to Lorraine, she said I should do it for the experience of public speaking, a skill I would be able to use later. Lorraine saw it as something that would help my development, and she was right on! That low-risk experience prepared me for my future jobs as an engineer, manager, salesperson, and community leader.

The next job Vern asked me to do was to teach a teen Sunday School class in comparative religions. There was no classroom space available, but he came up with the idea to use the steps leading down to the furnace room. The students could sit on the steps in pairs and I could stand at the bottom facing them. Again, I talked this request over with Lorraine and she thought she could find a place to wait with Elizabeth on Sunday mornings until I was done.

Vern provided the teaching material and the class grew to fill the steps available. One Sunday morning, Vern announced, from the pulpit, that he would be starting an evening class for new members who were not familiar with the Lutheran liturgy. That sounded like the help I needed to give me more confidence teaching my Sunday morning class. Again, Lorraine encouraged me to do it, so I signed up.

During one of those sessions, Vern told the class that if we just believed that Jesus was God's son and accepted Him as our personal savior, we would be saved for eternity. Wow! That was a better deal than what I understood. I had believed that when I died, I would be examined at the pearly gates to see what kind of life I had lived before I could be admitted into heaven. I was so excited to get home and tell Lorraine what I learned in Vern's class.

Lorraine was way ahead of me spiritually. She said, "I

learned that in confirmation. What were you doing in your confirmation classes?" I said, "Our pastor was so dull and boring that we didn't pay much attention." That lesson hit me so hard that I made certain on Sunday mornings that my students clearly understood this good news.

One of my Sunday School students was David Olson. David had been active in Boy Scouts, and I had a background in Scouting. When I reached the age of twelve, I was eligible to join the Boy Scouts, and after a few years of earning the required merit badges, I attained the rank of Life Scout. Sadly, I did not make Eagle Scout because I could not pass the swimming merit badge requirement. In the summer months, we were always at the cabin my father bought on the Mississippi River near Wacouta. My brother Keith and I spent our summers fixing problems there instead of swimming. The only time we got into the lake was to clean up for supper after spending the afternoon cutting down dead trees, splitting the wood for the fireplace in Cannon Falls, and grubbing out stumps with help from our beloved step-grandfather Jasper Grisim, Viola's elderly retired father.

St. Timothy Church sponsored a Boy Scout troop, but there were several boys who were past that stage in their lives, so the Scouting Committee decided to organize an Explorer Scout troop for the older boys. I was asked if I would be their leader and I agreed to take on the responsibility with help promised from members of the church's Scouting Committee.

Quite a few years later, I received a phone call from David Olson. He asked if I would be available to read several bible verses at his ordination service. He had recently completed his course work at Luther Seminary in St. Paul to become a pastor! I asked, "Why me, David?" He said, "Because you were such a strong influence in my life." I replied, "Yes, David, I will do that, I feel honored that you have asked me." We have since stayed in touch. David is now a Bishop in the ELCA. It shows that one never knows how you may influence a young person at some moment in their life.

Years later, my daughter Susan would serve on the board of directors of Luther Seminary. When she was introduced, another board member got a twinkle in his eye and said, "I used to babysit you!" It was David Olson.

Chapter 8

THE ROSEVILLE YEARS
1953-1958

On November 7, 1953, Lorraine and I moved into the first place we could really call *home*. The house at 2782 Dellwood was in a growing neighborhood in Roseville with preschool kids in every house. Daughter Elizabeth had her choice of playmates. St. Timothy Church was just a short drive away, so we continued our membership there.

During this time, Susan was born on June 12, 1955, in the Red Wing City Hospital. I will never forget that night because I didn't get back home until the wee hours of the morning. I was so tired that when I closed the garage door my hand got caught between the panels of the door. The pain knocked me to the ground and I just rolled around and moaned until I realized I needed to get Elizabeth inside and into bed.

Susan was baptized in our new house by Pastor Anderson on June 12, 1955. As with her sister, Susan's sponsors were her Aunt Florraine, and Uncle Keith.

In 1958, we decided to move from our house in Roseville primarily because we had outgrown it after Paul was welcomed to our family on October 21, 1957. There were only two bedrooms on the first floor, and we decided not to improve the basement to put our children down there where we couldn't hear them if they became sick.

About that same time, I was growing weary of my long

commute to work and home again in rush-hour traffic. After many days of driving around to look at houses and hearing the kids whine, "When are we going home?" we bought a newly built house at 5024 Valley View Road in Edina.

they're building PROFIT-POWER into this electronic brain

Univac File-Computer will open up a vast new world of profits because it will . . .

* whip through your routine accounting chores in a fraction of the time, for a fraction of the cost.
* keep full, up-to-the-moment records on large volumes of fast-moving items or accounts.
* provide fast, accurate answers to your vital profit & loss questions—guide management action.
* furnish you with large-scale surveys and reports impossible with conventional methods.

Why not let us *show* you how the PROFIT-POWER of Univac File-Computer can help you reduce costs . . . seize opportunities . . . please customers . . . get the jump on competition. Call your local branch or write for free folder: "A Big New Step Toward the Automatic Office," *today*, Room 1916, 315 Fourth Ave., New York 10.

UNIVAC®
FILE-COMPUTER

Remington Rand Univac
DIVISION OF SPERRY RAND CORPORATION

Jerry in a Remington Rand Univac advertisement, Newsweek, Sep. 1956

My Salaried Jobs During the Years 1951-1958

Engineering Research Associates (ERA) / UNIVAC, St. Paul, Minnesota

In 1952, Remington Rand acquired ERA, and renamed it UNIVAC. In 1955, Remington Rand/Univac was acquired by Sperry Corporation. During my seven years at Univac, I was given complete freedom for design innovation. I was the first engineer to replace vacuum tubes and relays with transistors. As a result of my work, I was granted three U.S. patents. I also had the privilege of working side by side with some of the notable pioneers of the computer industry – the most famous being Seymour Cray, known as the "father of supercomputing."

A Payroll Panic at Cutler Hammer Company, Milwaukee, Wisconsin

My supervisor, Robert (Bob) Erickson called me into his office to tell me about a phone conversation he was having with our Univac Customer Engineer at Cutler Hammer in Milwaukee. It was payday there and they were unable to extract the necessary data from the computer to print paychecks. When Bob handed the phone to me the customer engineering tech told me he was trying to identify why the data was not appearing. Apparently, his scope probe had slipped and made an accidental connection that erased the timing track. I said, "No problem, there is a spare timing track." He said he accidently erased that one also. "Oh!" I told Bob, "This is serious!"

To write a timing track in the factory, the technicians use a six-foot-high rack of equipment that cannot be transported in an airplane seat. I thought perhaps my personal Heathkit audio generator at home could be adjusted to the correct frequency and copied to the recording head. With that idea, I was on the first flight to Milwaukee the next morning.

I was met at the airport and taken to the customer site. I connected my audio generator to one input of the dual-trace oscilloscope and the second probe to a data track. It was soon apparent to everyone that my generator was not stable enough to write a usable timing track.

Taking a step back, I saw there was another drum in that cabinet, so I re-connected the scope probe from my generator to the timing track of the second drum. There was a slight difference of speed between the two drums so I held my handkerchief against the protruding shaft of the faster drum and found I could synchronize the two drums perfectly. The technician then rigged up a cable to connect from the read head of the second drum's timing track to a write head on the defective drum with a push button. Everybody got ready so when the drums were synchronized, I yelled, "PUSH!" And we were done.

The tech straightened up the site and told the computer users the payroll data should be available. We went out for a cup of coffee and they took me to the airport. When I got back to the office and told Bob the story, he said, "Jerry, write that up and I'll see that it gets into the user manuals and a service bulletin to all the file-computer sites."

At Univac, I gained a lot of knowledge about digital technology, the importance of engineering documentation, thorough design testing, and most importantly, the value of customer involvement and support for new product development. Undoubtedly, the greatest lesson I learned during my time at Univac is that management must be visible and demonstrate its interest in all phases of a company's business. If Sperry Corporation management had done that, there probably wouldn't have been a company called Control Data.

At Univac, I had the opportunity to observe how morale can completely disintegrate when top-level management shows no interest in the employees or their work. I saw how a company can be torn apart by political infighting. My supervisor, Bob Erickson, called me into his office to tell me Bill Norris was leaving his job as manager of the St. Paul Univac operation to start a new computer company. If Bill Norris decided to walk away from the fight, it was time for me to explore new possibilities too.

Soon after this, a salesman named Don Hamilton called on me at Univac. I told him I was looking for a new job. One night after supper, Don called me at home to say he was thinking of starting a new company to manufacture products his customers were unable to get through the companies he represented. Don asked if I'd be interested to help get this business started. I was definitely interested. That business became Transistor Electronics Corporation.

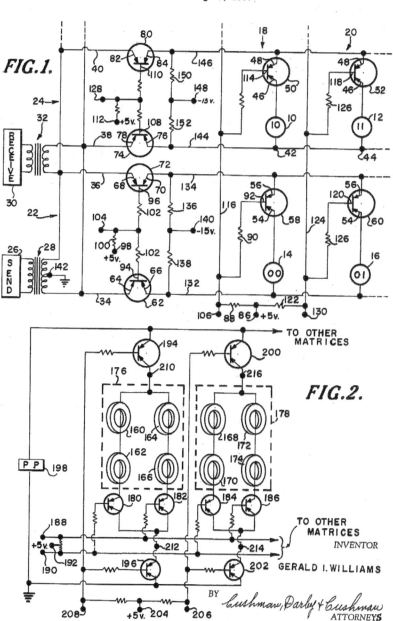

FIG.1.

FIG.2.

TO OTHER MATRICES

TO OTHER MATRICES

INVENTOR

GERALD I. WILLIAMS

BY

Cushman, Darby & Cushman
ATTORNEYS

Chapter 9

THE EDINA YEARS
1958-1987

These were some of the best years for my young family. We moved from our house in Roseville to Edina in the fall of 1958. A contractor had been building the walk-out rambler-style house at 5024 Valley View Road for his own family. He was short of cash and needed to sell something to keep his business going, so we bought it from him, and it suited us very well for the next three decades.

The new house had three bedrooms on the first floor, but one was quite small so after a few years we opted to finish the lower level

5024 Valley View Road, Edina

with a large bedroom and a three-quarter bathroom for Elizabeth and Susan to share. I built in two closets and a double-desk area for studying. There were two large windows fitted with interior shutters for natural light and privacy.

The builder added a fireplace in part of the lower level intended to be a recreation room. We finished that area with acoustical tile on the ceiling, gray barn-siding for wainscoting, black felt-covered "bulletin boards" above for posters or other displays, and red brick-patterned vinyl tile on the floor. The space was large enough for a ping-pong table and we installed a roll-up projection screen on one wall for viewing slides.

Some of the remaining basement space became Lorraine's sewing/laundry room and a small storeroom for canned goods. I enjoyed installing cabinets and a smooth white countertop for her. The workshop had two workbenches – one for Paul and one for me. This shop became the birthplace of many radio-controlled model airplanes and ultimately of Williams Sound Corp.

Ours was the only house on the block when we moved in, with the exception of an abandoned old place next door that could have served as a spooky house for a movie. It was torn down soon after we got settled. I was able to salvage some of the large limestone foundation blocks to build a retaining wall in our backyard with steps up to a garden area where Lorraine planted flowers and herbs.

Hennepin County decided the southern suburbs of Minneapolis needed a major east-west thoroughfare and selected West 62nd Street to become a freeway. It was several months before it was completed, so folks used it for bicycle riding. We bought bikes for the whole family and went riding almost every evening after supper. Lorraine really enjoyed it because this was the first bike she had ever owned, and she mastered it very quickly. The new road was named Minnesota Highway 62.

Our family trip to Colonial Williamsburg at Christmas time in 1965 inspired Lorraine to redecorate our house. In an effort to get just the right shade of blue in our living room, one wall was repainted three times! I was inspired to recreate the charm of candles in each window for the front of our house for Christmas lighting, so I mounted electric candles on wooden boards and stained them to match the interior windowsills. The current was adjusted to match the brightness of candlelight. Lorraine used that Christmas lighting all 30 years we lived in the house.

The Edina public school system had a reputation for excellence that proved true while Elizabeth, Susan and Paul attended. The music department was recognized as one of the best in Minnesota. Elizabeth began flute lessons in 5th grade and as a high schooler earned a spot in the top band. She was frequently invited to play solos in church – an experience that gave special meaning to her practice. Susan enjoyed singing in choirs in school and church. While living in Edina I developed audio recording capability to record choirs, bands, and soloists in the area and had those tapes turned into 33 1/3 records. Recording the high school concerts and editing the reel-to-reel tapes was a labor of love.

Moved to below

Our children wanted a pet, but Susan's allergy to cats and most dogs restricted the kind of pet we could have, so we tried tropical fish. The kids, particularly Susan, enjoyed the experience, but they really wanted a furry animal they could cuddle. I built a rabbit hutch and we acquired three Dutch rabbits, one for each kid. Elizabeth named hers Ginger, Susan's was Pepper, and Paul came up with the name Frisky Nibble for his, after the girls nixed his first choice of "Tugboat."

The rabbits satisfied them for a while, but what they really wanted was a pet they could have a relationship with. Dr. Stoesser, our allergist, suggested a poodle because they do not shed. We found a black miniature poodle we named Williams' Wee Willie, and he was just right for our family. Willie was a smart dog. When we discussed who was going to take him for his evening walk, we could not use the word because he would get so excited. When we started spelling out w-a-l-k, he figured what that meant out too!

One of the best things I ever did in our home was hire a cabinet maker to convert our rectangular kitchen table into a round table. That meant that we were all equal. We had very interesting discussions around our supper table, which frequently motivated one of us to jump up to get a volume of World Book encyclopedia to settle a question.

Our living and dining room in the front of the house had low windows facing the street. When it was time for me to come home from work, Willie watched for my car and when he saw it, he ran to the door expecting to be petted as soon as I walked in, which I usually did. One evening, Lorraine challenged me why Willy got petted before she got a kiss. I made a comment like, "I think you need to get to the head of the line." That was not a good response.

When Lorraine was in her early thirties, she was struck with severe rheumatoid arthritis. Despite the pain, she tried valiantly to maintain her normal activities with a husband and three school-aged children, but there were days when even getting out of bed was more than she could manage. Of course, this was devastating to her and challenging for the whole family, but Lorraine remained a wonderful wife and mother.

Transistor Electronics Corp, St. Louis Park, 1958-1963

In the fall of 1958, I was invited to participate in forming a new company to be called Transistor Electronics Corporation. TEC was being organized to develop and manufacture complex components for the computer industry – items needed in designing transistor technology into computers. Those components were not available in the marketplace at that time.

Don Hamilton, the president of TEC, was a man with excellent marketing skills, so the business developed very quickly. However, I was driving twenty miles to work across town before there were any freeways, so Lorraine and I

★ ★ ★ ★   ★ ★ ★ ★

THE ELECTRONICS game today has such potential that Gerald I. Williams, one of the youngest idea men in the play, feels he's "limited only by my imagination."

Williams, 31 years old, is vice president and chief engineer for the eight-month-old Translator Electronics Corp., St. Louis Park, which makes parts and testing equipment for electronic computers.

Gerald Williams

He's in an executive position at an early age because he got an early start. He was only 14 in his native Cannon Falls, Minn., when he got a part time job as an electrician's helper and appliance repairman.

This was while he was winning top scholastic honors in high school and awards from the National Honor society and American Legion, and playing end on the football team.

He rounded out his training as a navy radar man, engineer for WCAL, Northfield, while working his way through a two-year study at St. Olaf college, and University of Minnesota, where he got his electrical engineering degree in 1950.

He had his professional upbringing with Zenith Radio Corp., Engineering Research Associates and Remington Rand Univac.

Williams, who recently moved from St. Paul to 5024 Valley View Rd., Edina, was a charter member of St. Timothy Lutheran church, St. Paul, was a member of the board of deacons three years and superintendent of the senior Sunday school department.

He also organized a Boy Scout troop and an Explorer Scout post. His other interests are fishing, skiing, photography and hi-fi. Williams and his wife, Lorraine, have three children, Elizabeth, 6; Susan, 3, and Paul, 8 months.

decided to look for a house nearer to TEC. I believe God led us to that house in Edina. It was across the street from Normandale Lutheran Church.

When we moved in, ours was the only house on the street for three blocks. Our closest neighbors were Pastor Don Carlson, and his wife Marie, who lived in the church parsonage adjacent to Normandale Lutheran Church, kitty-corner across the street from our house. Their children, David, Dan, and Ruth were convenient and favorite baby-sitters for our kids.

While they were great neighbors, we had belonged to ALC Lutheran churches since we were married, and Normandale was an LCA (Swedish) Lutheran congregation. Upon returning home one Sunday after visiting yet another ALC church, Lorraine said, "Jerry, I think we should join Normandale, because when the kids are in confirmation it will be easier to send them across the street instead of driving them to another church."

We soon found ourselves teaching Sunday School and involved in other church activities. But the president of TEC, who also belonged to that church, told me not to get too involved because he wanted me to put all my effort into the company. He even warned the pastor not to make any demands on me.

I chose to ignore that warning because I felt that I had to put my commitment to God ahead of my commitment to my employer. The Bible says in Joshua 24:15, "Choose this day whom you will serve. As for me and my house, we will serve the Lord." We continued to be involved at the church, and the company prospered too. The president became a very wealthy man in a few years, and we were also blessed financially.

At TEC I was free to pursue anything that looked like a good opportunity, beginning with managing the engineering activity, later manufacturing, and ultimately the entire operation. I also received formal training in business management at the American Management Association in New York. However, after one of my New York trips I observed that success was taking its toll on the president in terms of his health and personal relationships. In my opinion, the president had begun to honor wealth and power and was turning his back on God and the people who had worked to build the business.

Friction started to develop between us, and it became apparent that we had fundamental differences over the future direction of TEC. As Lorraine and I and several of the directors of the company pondered the situation, I recalled a prayer-poem by Reinhold Niebuhr that says, "God grant me the serenity to accept the things I cannot change; the courage to change the things I can; and the wisdom to know the difference."

I made a painful, but peace-filled choice. The hours of night work, the weeks and weekends spent away from the family, the struggle to reach the top of an industry which offered a bright financial future, all of that work that had finally begun to pay off, was discarded in a simple letter of resignation. I felt guilty about deserting the good people I had hired and helped to develop. The act of emptying out my desk, taking down my personal pictures, walking out and locking the front door of the building that I had helped to plan and build, after everyone else had left for the weekend, is a feeling I will never forget.

Control Data Corporation (CDC), Bloomington, 1963-1979

Once again, I learned God provides opportunities and helps us rebuild our lives. Isaiah 40:31 says, "But they who wait upon the Lord shall renew their strength, they shall mount up with wings like eagles, they shall run and not be weary, they shall walk and not faint."

I never believed in burning bridges. I think Lorraine convinced me of that. In this case, many of the friends I had at Univac were now working at Control Data and they encouraged me to join them. One of those friends was Bill Keye, one of my higher-level supervisors at Univac. He had become Vice-President for Engineering at Control Data. After Bill took me on a tour of the company's plants, he gave me a choice of several opportunities. I was most impressed with the Cedar Engineering Division that manufactured precise miniature motors. This division was a leader in that field.

Bill explained that Control Data was having trouble with some of their outside suppliers of components. One example of such trouble was the quality and high cost of voltage-regulated DC power supplies. This was technology with which I was familiar. I told Bill I could start with that project while I got acquainted with the company's out-of-town divisions to see what other products should be considered.

The division I created to design and build the power supplies soon proved successful. The next project was to produce a multilayer printed circuit board. To do this, Control Data acquired a local fledgling company that had good technical talent but lacked the resources to produce a satisfactory product on time.

105

CDC provided the needed equipment to this new operation and with support from the division that needed that circuit board, employee morale was bolstered. It was soon delivering a quality product.

The positive results of those two enterprises caught the attention of Dr. John Baird, Vice President of Research and Development at the corporate level. He invited me to join his staff to establish an organization to assist the various engineering organizations to work together to improve the quality and reliability of the company's products while simultaneously reducing cost. We gradually built up a respected staff and an offering of services so after three years we had close to sixty people in the organization. Then, because of severe competitive pressure, CDC had a bad business year and I was told to cut twenty people from my staff. That was a heart-rending task.

Director of Engineering Standards

Because my new job title was General Manager of Technical Standards, I explored how CDC could collaborate with its competitors to develop standards that would allow their computers to interconnect. The initial emphasis was to interconnect with IBM machines.

That led me to an existing industry organization known as CBEMA, the acronym for the Computer and Business Equipment Manufacturers Association. I persuaded the higher management of CDC to join the group. When CDC joined CBEMA, we were introduced to ANSI, the American National Standards Institute. ANSI made me aware of the Computer

Standards Working groups that were already developing the first American Standard for Information Interchange that became known in time as ASCI.

ANSI welcomed me as Control Data's representative and assigned me to the Computer Standards Planning and Priorities Committee which was just getting underway. At the first meeting I attended, the IBM representative nominated me to be chairman. To my surprise I was elected unanimously. The next year I was re-elected without discussion.

As a result of this responsibility, I became the de facto representative for the United States on the International Standards Organization (ISO). Meetings were infrequent, but always in wonderful places like England, the Netherlands, Germany, France, and Italy. I bought plane tickets for Lorraine so she could accompany me on these trips.

Jerry and Lorraine in Germany

About that same time, Control Data formed a product-interchange relationship with the nationalized British and French computer companies so we could buy and sell products with them. It was called Multinational Data. Our meetings rotated between the U.S., England, and France.

The upper-level managers of these companies wanted written standards to ensure trouble-free interconnection of the three companies' products, so I attended the meetings of the English and French companies. Each company tried to out-do the other with hospitality. When the meetings were held in England, Jerry Woolsey, the English representative, insisted I stay at his charming cottage home in Great Gransden near Cambridge. His wife, Jacquie, was a wonderful hostess. Lorraine especially enjoyed our visits with the Woolseys. Our conversations were great fun because we discovered a number of words have different meanings in British and American English. Once during a committee meeting, the Englishmen suggested that we "table" a very important discussion. We Americans were baffled – until we realized that "to table" an item in England meant putting it on the agenda, not delaying it until the next meeting.

Around 1974, I attended a planning meeting of Control Data's upper-level management for the computer division. Whoever was chairing the meeting said, "We build the biggest, fastest computers in the world, and that's what we're going to keep on doing." I stood up and said, "You guys don't know where this world is going. When memory becomes more affordable there will be computers on every desk and there won't be enough work for these dinosaurs that we're building." Another man stood up and said, "Jerry, I've known you for about fifteen years, and that's the dumbest thing I've ever heard you say." That's when the meeting ended. Four years later Control Data closed its doors permanently as desk-top computers took over.

In the mid-1970s the United States was hit with an economic recession. A few weeks before Christmas I was told another twenty people had to be let go. The recession continued and two years later, my boss, Bob Perkins who was Vice President for Engineering, called me into his office to tell me that pressure from the banking institutions was forcing another work force reduction. His job had been abolished along with the jobs of the other two men who reported to him. I was the only one on his staff to survive that cut, but the price I had to pay was to cut my staff from twenty people down to ten. My heart was heavy. The apostle Paul wrote in his letter to the Philippians, "Have no anxiety about anything but in everything, by prayer and supplication with thanksgiving, let your request be made known to God. And the peace of God which passes all understanding will keep your hearts and minds in Christ Jesus."

As I walked back to my office, I pondered that verse. Jesus told the people when they pray, they should go into their room and shut the door and pray to the Father in secret and the Father who sees in secret will reward them. When I got back to my office, I closed the door and fell down on my knees against a chair and took my concern to God.

I prayed God would help me find jobs for all those people and that none of them should be anxious or upset. I went to each of the ten privately and told them what was happening and that I had already asked God for help to find them a new opportunity. One person doubted and quit. During the next few months, nine of them got better paying jobs within the company than they had on my staff. One of the nine thought that he was out for certain when, on his last day no job had come through. I never doubted God though, and at 3:30 that afternoon, an offer came for him. He could scarcely believe it, but I could.

As pleased as I was at how, with the help of God, each of those people got new jobs, I was equally distressed that the company had showed so little concern for my three colleagues. Each had distinguished themselves with substantial technical and managerial contributions for the company. I decided I had better start building an "ark" or at least a small lifeboat before the next crisis, because they seemed to be coming more frequently.

Normandale Lutheran Church, 1959-1987

After moving to Edina, we visited perhaps four or five congregations on Sunday mornings including Mount Olivet in south Minneapolis, the largest Lutheran church in the Twin Cities. I've already explained a bit about how and why we chose to join Normandale Lutheran Church. I don't recall what we did with the children during those church visits in 1959. At the time, Elizabeth was seven years old, Susan was four, and Paul was only one. So, we joined Normandale. At the time, I believe the membership was only about 200 souls. By the time Lorraine and I moved to Lake Hubert 29 years later in 1987, Normandale's membership had then grown tenfold!

During our time at Normandale Lutheran Church, we became deeply immersed in the activities of the congregation. Because of insufficient room in the church building in 1958, one or two Sunday School classes met in the basement of our house across the street until the first church addition was completed. I designed and installed the first sound system in the newly completed sanctuary with a microphone control panel on the back

Normandale Lutheran Church sound control panel

of the 4th pew on the south side. Until I was able to train others, I was the sole operator.

When Sunday School enrollment reached 300 children, I became the first superintendent. I finished the space under the stairway to the sanctuary with shelves for the teachers' baskets of supplies. Until the congregation was able to hire its first full-time Christian Education Director, Miss Irene Getz, I recruited all the Sunday School teachers by visiting them in their homes. I introduced the Bethel Bible Series Curriculum to Pastor Carlson. Both Lorraine and I taught classes.

Bob Peterson and I introduced Pastor Carlson to Men's Bible Study Fellowship (BSF) Program when the class attended at Mt. Olivet Church was about to lose its space in that church. Pastor Carlson welcomed BSF to Normandale. That weekly study was responsible for many families joining our church and for saving many souls. When new families moved into our neighborhood, I was frequently asked, "What goes on at your church on Monday nights?" When I responded, "It is a men's Bible study class," the typical response was, "Yeah, but what else is going on?" They asked because cars were parked up and down the streets for several blocks. There were about 600 men attending those evening classes with a waiting list to get in.

I was devoting so much of my time to the church that one

night at the supper table, Paul asked if I was going to my office tonight. That remark was a clue that perhaps I should be home more in the evenings.

When Pastor Carlson nominated Lorraine for the church council at a congregational annual meeting, she became the first woman ever elected to the Normandale Church Council. After that, women were regularly nominated and elected. I served several terms on the council as well.

I chaired the Church Planning Committee for the first major building project and served on two more building committees. Lorraine and I and another couple repainted the Fellowship Hall to make it more suitable for two wedding receptions planned for that year – Elizabeth's and the pastor's daughter, Ruth.

All three of our children were involved in choir, participated in youth activities, and were confirmed in their faith at Normandale.

Williams Family, 1967

A year or so before that last round of layoffs at Control Data one of the couples in our church came to the pastor and told him their elderly mother, Ellen, was unable to hear his sermons because of her hearing impairment. The pastor relayed their request to me since I had designed and installed the sound system in the church.

Ellen was eighty-three years old and used a hearing aid that worked quite well for her in most settings. However, in large gatherings such as a worship service in a reverberant space her hearing aid masked the voice of the pastor by primarily amplifying the noises around her. The family asked if I could install some jacks on the back of a pew where Ellen could plug in a pair of headphones.

I had installed headphones and jacks in the pews of other churches but observed that very few people used them. There seemed to be a stigma attached to those pews, the "deaf rows." I told the family I would not install such a system in our church. However, I was thinking about trying the recently introduced low-cost transistor AM radio in conjunction with a specialized transmitter attached to the church's sound system. That way Ellen could sit wherever she chose, take the little radio out of her purse, put in a small earphone, and adjust the volume to suit her needs.

Ellen was eager to try this experiment. I built a transmitter using some spare parts and several vacuum tubes that were lying around my home workshop. I bought a little Sony pocket receiver, removed the loudspeaker, and fixed the station selector to the frequency of my homemade transmitter.

Then I tried it out for a couple of Sundays. In the course of checking out the system, I got a few strange looks and comments from some friends who thought I might be listening to the Twins ballgame during the sermon. The following week I gave it to Ellen and showed her how to use it.

When I approached her after the service to ask how it worked, she started to cry. When I asked her why she was crying, she said it was the first time she had heard the sermon in the three years she had been attending our church. Her daughter asked me to supply receivers to several other people who had a similar problem, which I did.

This inspired the birth of Williams Sound Corp.

Williams Sound Corp, Edina/Eden Prairie, 1975-1987

Having survived the layoffs at Control Data, Lorraine and I discussed some possibilities should I be forced to look for another job soon. One way I could directly serve God with my technical talent would be to meet the need for churches to help people hear the Word of God. Since my job at Control Data wasn't in imminent danger, we were slow to take action, until one day a friend, Herb Streitz, who was in the recording business, stopped by to have me calibrate his equipment. He asked what was new in my life.

I told Herb about the wireless hearing support system idea and he said he was planning an advertising mailing in the fall to two thousand churches in Minnesota, Iowa, and Wisconsin. He would gladly enclose a piece of my literature in his mailing. I said, "Herb, it's just an idea. I don't have literature or even a product suitable for sale yet." As Herb left, he said I should keep his offer in mind.

Lorraine and I thought Herb's proposal was an ideal opportunity to test the market. I drafted a letter that began, "Dear

Pastor," in which I described the concept of the system, gave approximate costs, and asked them to write to me if the idea interested them. I went on to say that if there is sufficient response, I would invest my time and money to develop and p roduce the product. I sent the letter to Herb and he replied that he would reprint the letter and enclose it in his mailing.

That mailing went out in late October 1974 and responses started to come in one by one. It dawned on me that we would be faced with a decision – how many letters would it take for us to proceed? Knowing I needed help, I called a boyhood schoolmate, Allen Anderson, who was in the advertising business in Minneapolis.

After describing everything to Allen, I asked, "What kind of response can I expect from this mailing?" It was Allen's turn to ask the questions. "Did you enclose pictures of the product?" No. Did you give firm prices?" No. "Did you enclose a business reply card?" No. He said, "You mean that you expect people to pick up pen and paper and write you a letter?" Yes. He said, "You're crazy! When we use direct mail and do everything right, we're happy if we get a one percent response. You'll be lucky if you get anything back!" I responded, "But I already have several letters," to which he countered, "Well that's probably all you'll get."

Needless to say, as I drove back to Control Data I was dis-couraged that I had not done a very good job of using Herb's generous offer. I decided to take the question to God in prayer. After all, a one percent response didn't seem like much. That would only be twenty responses from the 2,000 pieces mailed.

I remembered the fleece test Gideon put before God to prove to himself that God would support his battle plan to defend Israel. It is described in Judges 6:37-40.

Knowing the time and money it would take to develop and promote this new product I wanted that same confidence so Lorraine would also be convinced, because this project would require sacrifice and involvement on her part.

In my prayer, I told God if I had a one percent return on the mailing – twenty letters, I would proceed. If not, I would drop the project and not be disappointed. After several weeks I had received a number of letters. Pastors wrote this product would be an answer to prayers for their members and they hoped we could help them.

Lorraine met me at the airport after I had been out of town for a week on business and handed me several letters. She told me to read them during the drive home because these were particularly encouraging. We now had a total of sixteen responses. I was so excited I called Herb to ask how many flyers he had sent out, because that number would be significant. He said he had mailed 1,615 pieces.

I turned to Lorraine and said, "That's it!" We have sixteen letters and that's the one percent that I had asked God for. She surprised me when shook her finger at me and said, "No, your deal with the Lord was twenty letters. You wait."

For once in my life I did the right thing and bit my tongue. I knew God would be faithful and not let this divide us, so I said, "Okay, I'll wait. If God wants us to do this, He's not going to let four letters stand in the way." Guess what happened the next week? No letters. But on Saturday, I wasn't feeling well and stayed in bed. Lorraine walked in and said she had something to cheer me up as she handed me four more letters! I don't mind admitting I was so happy I cried. I learned we can pray and hope for answers, even if we sometimes lack faith that our prayers will be answered.

Decision Point: 1974

With Christmas just a few days away, we put the project out of our minds until the 7th of January when another letter arrived. It was from one of the twenty responding churches asking how our survey had turned out. It was time to make a decision. I had made a commitment to God: if my prayer for twenty letters was answered we would proceed with the project. Lorraine agreed my prayer had been answered in the affirmative, so we wrote to the twenty churches that we were going ahead.

Now I felt real responsibility. We had to use the best technology available to create a reliable system in full accordance with Federal Communications Commission regulations. Some of the design requirements were in technical areas where I had little or no experience.

Proverbs 3:5-6 says, "Trust in the Lord with all your heart and do not rely on your own insight. In all your ways acknowledge Him and he will make straight your paths." Comforted by those words, I talked to anyone I thought could help me technically, got some books on the latest solid-state radio transmitter technology, and contacted the local FCC office for their guidance.

117

By August 1975, I installed a clearer, stronger transmitter in Normandale Church to replace the earlier vacuum tube transmitter. Parts were ordered to make one hundred more systems and we advertised in two national magazines mailed to pastors and church administrators. I also ordered a subscription to the FCC regulations to keep up with any changes.

Trouble with the FCC

In December, as components were arriving, so did a revision to the FCC rules. The rules had changed to require unlicensed low-power transmitters be tested and the results sent to the commission before any marketing could commence.

I was already in trouble with the very agency whose support I needed. I called the local FCC office and told them I was in violation of the new rule because we had already scheduled advertising. They said, "Don't worry, just call the Washington people. We've got more to do than to worry about people who are trying to conform with the rules." I called the Washington people. They said the same thing and just asked that we get the testing done and send the results as soon as possible.

The rule change affected some of the technical requirements. After some redesigning of the transmitter I arranged for testing by a local laboratory. The results were sent to the FCC. While we waited for certification, we started building the first dozen systems to meet the orders that were coming in one by one. A few weeks later, Lorraine called me at the office to tell me a letter from the FCC said they rejected our request for certification.

It came down to an interpretation of one requirement that was a bit ambiguous. The FCC engineer suggested I re-apply under another procedure that required field strength measurements be made in an open area outside the building in which the transmitter operated at a distance of 300 meters (1000 feet). I had avoided that procedure for obvious reasons to anyone familiar with Minnesota winters, but now it was March and the snow was nearly gone so that we could proceed with the tests. Regrettably, I found I had to reduce the power of the transmitter to comply with the rules, which in turn reduced its useful range.

With new results in hand, I flew to the FCC laboratories in Laurel, Maryland. I had some concerns. Would I be able to restore the transmitter's power? Would the FCC be supportive? I took a few minutes to pray and told God it was up to Him to make this trip pay off. I knew He had led us this far and He wouldn't let me down, but the trip had not been smooth. Because of bad weather in Chicago, I had missed my flight connection and got only three or four hours of sleep. I was very tired and needed reassurance.

My concern was all for nothing because the engineer who handled my request was a committed Christian and his wife used a hearing aid. He was completely sympathetic to my cause. He reviewed the test results and told me the changes I had made allowed for certification. He suggested I visit the FCC engineering office in Washington about the feasibility for a special ruling so that we could legally increase the power and range of our system.

A few weeks later on a second trip to Washington, I had the same apprehensions because the federal bureaucracy can be overwhelming to a neophyte. Again, I prayed that God would guide the discussion. There, in that big federal bureaucracy, I ended up talking to an engineer who allowed God to direct his life. He suggested I file a petition to establish a nationwide frequency for hearing assistance transmitters to operate with increased power. Needless to say, I walked out giving praise to God. The application was filed as suggested, but the FCC took no action until 1983, eight long years later.

A Business is Born, Williams Sound Corp, 1976

Meanwhile, orders were coming in and we began shipping systems. It was thrilling to receive letters telling how our product was helping people, but running a part-time business, in conjunction with my full-time job at Control Data placed extraordinary demands on my time. Amazingly, whenever

Lorraine at her Williams Sound desk in the basement rec room

we got a little behind, the incoming orders slacked off until we got caught up. God knew how much pressure we could manage, and He regulated it well.

We were depleting our inventory of receivers very quickly. The orders and the number of receivers per order were both increasing. We had a new problem – the receiver manufacturer discontinued the model we were using, and the replacement model was not adaptable to our needs. After taking this concern to God in prayer the direction I received seem to indicate I should go to Hong Kong where most pocket radios were being made. The Hong Kong yellow pages listed 179 radio manufacturers. I wrote down the names and addresses of forty. Which manufacturer would we best work with? I hoped something could be worked out in the ten vacation days I had budgeted for this trip.

I knew no one over there, so I started asking my Christian friends if they had any acquaintances I could call on if I needed help. I discovered the manager of the Billy Graham office in Hong Kong was an East Indian, who, as a student in Minneapolis, had come to our home a number of times for dinner. I also learned that one of my friends had a brother who was working there as a Lutheran missionary. These two contacts and others they introduced to me provided the solution to my quest. In the process, we developed a strong bond of Christian fellowship with them and their families, and they later felt free to ask me to help them with some favors that were within my ability to grant.

By October of that year, we had outgrown our basement space and moved the business into a business site in Eden Prairie. By devoting full-time to the business, it grew even more rapidly. By April 1986, we had about thirty-five employees, and had outgrown all the space available to us in that building. We moved to a new industrial office park in Minnetonka, where the company stayed several more years.

When Lorraine said we needed help in the office, we hired my former secretary from Control Data, Marilyn Benusa, on a short-term basis. Then came Mary Beth Scheid. Mary Beth recommended Barb Gudknect and Barb recom-

Jerry in front of Williams Sound

mended Kathy Ohama when I needed a full-time accountant. They added an air of professionalism to the company. Lorraine quit soon after those three ladies came to work because she felt she was no longer needed. That made for a better home life for both of us, because we both realized Williams Sound was at the "run stage" when we started getting orders from sound contractors who wanted to sell and distribute our product.

Our first contractor customer was Russ O'Toole from the Chicago area. I had to adjust our prices to allow him to make a profit. Russ, in turn, put us in touch with Paul and Marilyn Bunker who owned Sunrise Sales. They were manufacturers' representatives who had perhaps a dozen lines of commercial sound products. Again, we had to adjust our pricing to allow them to earn a commission, but that action opened the floodgates of orders. We added another sales representative, Irv Wolter, in the

Twin Cities.

Irv suggested we rent a booth at an audio trade show coming up in Las Vegas. I'll never forget it: Paul Ingebrigtsen and I sat on folding chairs at a card table on which we had one AM System displayed. Irv brought other reps to our table and then we were really off and running!

About that time, I began thinking about my earlier promise to Lorraine, that I would retire at age 60 if the Lord made it possible, but I would need someone to run the business. I mentioned to several people that I was looking for a CEO. My brother-in-law said he had a neighbor looking for a new job. His name was Jim Broz and the rest is bright history. I believe my angel had interceded again.

My son, Paul, and I had work benches on opposite walls in our basement shop at home. We also had a blackboard on the wall so whenever Paul had a question, we usually moved to the blackboard. We spent many hours together down there. Paul is very creative, and he read encyclopedias to put himself to sleep. He holds the only patent ever issued to Williams Sound (unless something else has been patented since I left). Paul's patent is for the plastic case design that is still in use for the PockeTalker Pro.

I will offer a bit of background on the PockeTalker. After Williams Sound had moved out of our house in Edina, I received several phone calls from pastors. The pattern was consistent: members of the congregation appreciated the receivers very much, but there was another need. When someone is admitted to the hospital their hearing aids are set aside so they won't get lost. This makes it difficult to have a meaningful visit without shouting. Could I make something for pastoral visits to people in the hospital?

I could usually satisfy those pastors by telling them to go to Radio Shack, but one pastor responded he had already been to Radio Shack and all they had was "junk."

That morning during coffee break, I mentioned this need to Dick Holmes. He said, "There's nothing to it. It's just the audio portion of our receiver. We'll just build in a mic preamp." Dick surprised me after lunch by handing me a working prototype! About 5:00, Paul Ingebrigtsen and I sat pondering how to market this new thing when my son Paul came along and asked, "What are you guys doing?" We showed him the prototype and he asked, "How does it work?" I said, "The pastor wears this amplifier in his shirt pocket with the mic sticking out and gives headphones to the patient so they can hear him." Paul suggested, "Why don't you call it the PockeTalker?" Not only does Williams Sound still make them, but a stylish new model has been released.

Ironically, after several subsequent moves to larger spaces, Williams Sound, now called Williams AV, is back on Valley View Road in Eden Prairie, just a short distance from its first location thirty-five years earlier.

Lorraine and I decided it was time to retire in 1987. In August, we sold Williams Sound to four of the employees, giving them four years to pay us out of the company's earnings. I am very proud of how this company continues to innovate and grow, and I am grateful to God for how He allowed me to help so many people through the gifts He gave me.

Chapter 10

THE LAKE HUBERT YEARS
1987-2007

After we moved to Edina, Lorraine wished for a summer lake home. I responded, "Lorraine, I am so busy with work I would not have enough time to take care of two places. But I will promise you this: when I retire, we will shop for a nice piece of lake property and build a nice retirement home."

When I reached retirement age in 1987, we sold Williams Sound to a group of our employees, by giving them four years to pay us out of the earnings of the company.

That all came to pass on schedule, so we began driving into northern Wisconsin on weekends looking for a nice lot on a good lake. We started looking in Wisconsin because we had enjoyed weekends on a lake near the town of Rice Lake where the Husos, one of the "potluck" couples, had hosted the group.

After a few jaunts in Wisconsin, we realized there were not many nice lakes that had a hospital nearby (important because Lorraine had developed complications with her arthritis), so we turned our search to Minnesota. We had friends at Normandale Church who owned cottages on Lake Hubert, near the city of Brainerd which had a first-class medical center and hospital, so we began our search there. A realtor was recommended to us. When he asked where we wanted to look, we said, "Lake Hubert." He replied that Hubert was the best lake in the Brainerd area and there isn't much available, but he would show us what he could.

We first saw an undeveloped lot with lots of birch and pine trees. It was about twelve feet higher than the lake. We looked at a few other possibilities but after supper in a restaurant we went back for another look at the first lot. A gentleman came out of his house and asked if we were interested in the lot. We replied yes, but we would prefer something a little lower to the lake because of Lorraine's physical limitations. His eyes lit up and he said he had a lower lot, but it was not yet listed. We asked to see it and immediately saw the possibilities, so we negotiated a deal for the lot, which was quite extensive with many dead trees still standing.

There was an old house on the adjacent property in which lived an elderly lady named Marion Kletchka. She invited us in for a visit and we learned Marion was a retired schoolteacher from Chicago who had married the man who owned the old house. She had a life estate in this summer place and a winter residence in Brainerd, about fifteen miles south. We assured her we were only interested in the vacant land.

Marian Kletchka and her Lake Hubert home

Lorraine had packed some clothes for us so we could stay in a motel, but Marion said we could sleep in her spare bedroom.

Lorraine wondered if we had time to go for a swim in the lake. When we came back up to the house, Marion invited us to stay for breakfast with her the next morning – she would bake rolls. That was an easy YES!

Lorraine and I had a lot to discuss on our way back to Edina. We were satisfied with the purchase and the pleasant lady next door. Now we needed to find an architect to design our house.

Hubert House in winter

"The Gardens of Jerry & Lorraine Williams"
– adapted from a handout for garden club tours

The home you are visiting is that of Jerry and Lorraine Williams on the east side of Lake Hubert. It was begun in May of 1987 and they moved into the house in February of 1988, although the final completion took much of the spring and summer of that year. Jerry, who is an electrical engineer, did much of the contracting, but the majority of the construction was

done by Nelson Brothers of Nisswa. The architect was Thomas
R. Blanck of St. Paul.

Lorraine wanted to build a
lodge-style home that looked as
though it had been on the lake
for many years. The architect has
done restoration work on many
of the older homes on Summit

Architect Tom Blanck

Avenue in St. Paul and understood the architectural style that
Lorraine wanted. The fact that he and Lorraine succeeded in
achieving a historic-looking house was attested to when the
elevator installer arrived toward the end of the construction and
asked how long we had been remodeling.

As you approach the home over the open bridge, notice
the Swedish rosemaling folk painting above the door. It was
done by Mr. Blanck's mother, Helen Elizabeth Blanck, who was

well- known as a
teacher and writer
of this method
of painting in the
Twin Cities. Sadly,
she passed away
six months after
completing it.

There are
many unique

Rosemaling over the front door

features in this home. It was built to accommodate handicapped people, so it has wide hallways, and doorways, raised toilets and an elevator between the main floor and lower floor, which exits at the lake level. A covered bridge with a ramp connects the garage to the home. The house has five extra bedrooms to accommodate the children and grandchildren during their visits. Jerry has three workshops, one for electronics, one for woodworking and one for greasy mechanical things.

The garage was painted with Swedish paint the Williams cooked on their kitchen stove. It is known by the name, falun rodt (red), from an area in Sweden where the special iron oxide powder is produced. The other ingredients are rye flour, linseed oil and water. The paint is claimed to last for up to 40 years. The house has a wood foundation and is heated with a groundwater heat pump. The annual heating and cooling costs are less than $900 per year.

The older cottage adjacent to the Williams' home was built around 1906 by a railroad man from Duluth and is one of the original houses on Lake Hubert. The Williams lived in that cottage during the construction of their new house.

The gardens were created in 1989 from the native woods, which came complete with underbrush and poison ivy. Lorraine had been the gardener in Edina until rheumatoid arthritis seriously limited her physical ability. Jerry's major contribution to yard maintenance in Edina had been mowing the lawn. At Lake Hubert, Lorraine participated by supervising the garden layouts while Jerry did the physical work.

The Williams first became interested in hostas about 1990, and in the fall of 1992 began a collection of hosta in a new garden that had previously been totally wild. The shade gardens display a collection of about 300 cultivars, specioids, and species hosta. Shade-loving companion plants included astilbe, dicentra, ferns, heuchera, pulmonaria, and annuals. Jerry started his impatiens and ageratum bedding plants from seed about April 1st to be set out about June 1st.

This area is in USDA zone 3B. The winter of 1995/1996 dipped to 41 degrees below zero. The soil was extremely sandy and required considerable amending which Jerry did with mulch made with his leaf shredder. The gardens are watered with water from Lake Hubert. It contains enough nutrient that very little fertilizer was needed.

Critters are always a problem – particularly deer, rabbits, chipmunks and raccoons. Jerry discovered a fertilizing product called Milorganite was the most effective repellent for the deer. The shady wooded setting of Lake Hubert House didn't lend itself easily to gardening, but the Williams discovered a love of

hosta. This took them to many garden tours in Minnesota and other states. They developed many friendships and Jerry began to enter his hosta in local shows. Eventually their gardens held 110 varieties. While in a plant nursery in 1995, Jerry noticed a sport with an unusually folded leaf. He

Praying Hands hosta

grew this odd hosta shoot and developed it into a new cultivar that was named "Praying Hands." It was named the American

Hosta Growers hosta of the year in 2011.

"Two Loons" – *from Lorraine's memorial service folder*

In December of 1984, after we bought our land on Lake Hubert, I was pondering what to get Lorraine for Christmas. It occurred to me how much she had come to love the loon calls during the late evening hours. So, I went to The Wooden Bird store and purchased the perfect gift for her: a painted hand-carved loon. The clerk did not have a suitable box so I told her to just put it in any container and I would find a box for it at my factory.

The next morning on my way to work my car was struck broadside by another car. Of course, there was a lot of damage to the car, but my greater concern was for the loon in the back seat. When I looked at it, I saw that the beak had been broken. I called The Wooden Bird store and asked if they could do a head transplant and the clerk assured me they could.

When I got home that evening, I told Lorraine about the accident with the car and explained that, unfortunately, her Christmas gift had been damaged too. But I quickly explained that the factory was in the Twin Cities and that it would be fixed by Christmas.

Well, that got her curiosity up. Unbeknownst to me, the next day she went through my dresser drawer until she found the sales slip. Lorraine later told me she had a big laugh over that because she had already bought a wooden loon exactly like it for my Christmas gift.

On Christmas Eve, she insisted that I open her gift to me

first. Imagine my surprise when I opened it. She laughed and then told me her story. She then suggested that we return one of the loons. But I said no, because loons are always paired up and these two loons would now represent the two of us together. They have been on our fireplace mantel ever since.

Good memories

Lorraine and I loved having our family come to stay for a few days, usually over a long holiday weekend. In the summer the kids and grandkids spent hours down at the lake, splashing in the water, catching minnows, and fishing. Fishing from the pontoon boat was always a special time, sometimes made even better by the loons that seemed to follow us. Susan's husband, Bob, became quite expert at finding the best fishing holes to catch bass.

The annual Fourth of July boat parade around the lake was another good time. After the kids decorated the pontoon boat with flags and streamers, we joined the line of decorated boats that slowly cruised the perimeter of the lake, all the while waving to our neighbors sitting at the shoreline. One year there were too many family members on the front end of the pontoon and the bow dipped down into the water. We almost lost a couple of kids that time!

Lorraine loved the lake

When Christmas was approaching, Lorraine insisted I find the tallest spruce tree that would fit in our lofty living room. Every year it was decked out with twinkling white lights, beautiful glass ornaments, and tinsel carefully hung one strand at a time. Lorraine always took special care with wrapping our gifts and her Christmas trees were worthy of being included in any decorator magazine. A sweet memory is the sight and sound of our young grandchildren, Svea, Sarah, Peter, Chris, and Kat serenading us from the walkway above the living room with carols on Christmas morning.

Losing Lorraine

Lorraine's health took a turn for the worst after Thanksgiving 2005. From then on, it was just a continual downhill slide that was hard to watch. Considering all that she had suffered, her spirit was amazingly good through February. Then we arranged for in-home hospice care. Early in the morning of 12 May 2006, I was awakened by the sound of heavy deep breathing and gasps for air coming from Lorraine in her bed next to mine. Was she breathing her last?

Some weeks before, during our bedtime prayer, Lorraine had asked the Lord how much longer she would need to endure the pain in her body. I followed up say, "Yes, Lord, she is ready to come to you. Please grant her request." Lorraine added, "Don't make fools of us, Lord!"

Now I went to get our daughter Susan from the guest room where she was sleeping. She had given me a week to be together for this moment that she apparently saw coming – a real gift to me. Susan immediately came to the bedroom. After she checked on Lorraine, she said, "Dad, there's no one home. She didn't even feel me pinch her." Together, we watched her breathe her last.

I went to the phone and called Karen, the LPN who had been caring for Lorraine for the past three years. When she arrived, she and Susan began dressing Lorraine's body, because they both said Lorraine wouldn't leave the house without wearing a nice outfit and her make-up. I called our doctor.

Lorraine had participated in planning her memorial service by writing her obituary and choosing the hymns and soloists. She had even planned her funeral lunch. Some years before, when the family was gathered at the hospital for one of Lorraine's surgeries, she told them if she didn't make it, she wanted her funeral luncheon cake to be a white sheet cake with yellow frosting, and a rosebud piped on each piece; she didn't want all the pretty frosting heaped up on one end of the cake. When the nurse came to let us know the surgery was successful and Lorraine was in recovery, Elizabeth cried out, "Cancel the sheet cake!"

Lorraine said she wanted her memorial fund used for new paraments for the church. Her wish

An example of the parament designed for Lutheran Church of the Cross

was carried out and they are spectacular.

Lorraine's memorial service folder

Lorraine was one of identical twin daughters born in St. James, Minnesota, on December 29, 1926, to Christian Henry and Emmy Helen (Schaper) Hoffman. She was raised in St. James, confirmed in the Christian faith at First Lutheran Church in St. James, and graduated from St. James High School in 1944. In the fall of 1944, Lorraine enrolled at St. Olaf College in Northfield and received her bachelor's degree in home economics in 1948. Upon graduation, she taught home economics at Truman, Minnesota, from 1948 to 1950.

Lorraine and Gerald Williams met in 1946 sitting next to each other in the St. Olaf band. On June 11, 1950, they were married at First Lutheran Church in St. James, in a double wedding with her twin sister, Florraine. She and Jerry raised two daughters, Elizabeth and Susan, and a son, Paul.

After a brief time in Chicago in 1951, they moved to Roseville, Minnesota. In 1958, they settled in Edina until 1987, when they retired to Lake Hubert, Minnesota. Lorraine supported Jerry in a business begun in 1976 that designed and built wireless hearing support systems for use in houses of worship. After just three years, the demand for their product made Williams Sound Corp. a full-time job for both of them. In 1987, they sold this very successful business to a group of their employees and built their retirement home on Lake Hubert, near Nisswa.

A committed full-time wife and mother, Lorraine was devoted to many interests, especially her children's activities and her church. She was a charter member of St. Timothy Lutheran Church in St. Paul. At Normandale Lutheran Church in Edina, she was president of the Normandale Lutheran Church Women, sang in the choir, taught Vacation Bible School, and was the first woman elected to the church council. At Lutheran Church of the Cross in Nisswa, she was active in the women's organization, taking a leadership role in planning the new kitchen in the Celebration Center. She was also an active member of the Nisswa Women's Club, the Nisswa Garden Club and the Lake Hubert Women's Club.

Lorraine was renowned for her talents as a cook, seamstress, and home decorator. She loved to read and travel, and particularly enjoyed stays in their Maui condominium. Regrettably, she was afflicted for 45 years with severe rheumatoid arthritis which sharply curtailed her activities in later years.

Lorraine died in her home on May 12, 2006, at the age of 79 after a prolonged illness. She is survived by Gerald, her husband of 56 years. Jerry, her family, and friends look forward to being greeted by her in heaven, happy, whole, and probably offering something delicious to eat.

Condominium at Maui, Hawaii

[The following has been updated as of September 2020.]

Her children are Elizabeth (Roger) Gomoll of St. Paul, Dr. Susan (Dr. Robert) Jenkins of Rochester, and Paul (Evone Greene) Williams of Rockford, Minnesota.

Her grandchildren are Svea (Dr. Stephen) Merry of Rochester; Sarah (Dr. Matthew) Beckman of State College, Pennsylvania; Peter (Betsy) Wall of Rochester; Christopher Jenkins of St. Paul; and Katherine (Samuel) Lauer of Minneapolis.

Her great-grandchildren are Matthew (Katie) Merry, and Marielle, Jonathan, Katianna, Benjamin, and Andrew Merry, Rochester; Eden, Jack, and Hazel Beckman, State College; and Grace and Zachary Wall, Rochester.

Her sister was Florraine (Dr. William) Trygstad of Hastings, Minnesota, and her brother was Waldo (Gail) Hoffman of Pleasant Hills, California.

Last photo of Florraine & Lorraine together, 2006

Our whole family loved "Hubert House," our Lake Hubert home and its idyllic location. It was a very sad day when Lorraine passed away, and her death changed everything. After being her caretaker for so many years, I would have to redefine myself and I soon realized I had to relocate because I did not want to live there alone.

Hubert House viewed from the lake

Chapter 11

MY NORTHFIELD RETIREMENT YEARS
2007-2020

Note: Much of the content for this chapter has been drawn from my annual Christmas letters.

One winter morning at Lake Hubert, I was awakened by my alarm clock. It was time to get up and get dressed to go to Lutheran Church of the Cross for Sunday morning worship service.

I looked out a window and realized I would need to plow the driveway before I could drive to church. While sitting atop my faithful John Deere tractor, I asked myself, "What am I doing living here alone in the north woods of Minnesota after Lorraine has died, and my neighbors are down south enjoying warmer weather?" It was a very lonely existence except for my little poodle, Fancie.

I had been invited by Jody (Florraine's daughter and my third daughter by marriage) to her house for our large family's Christmas celebration. It should be a fun-filled evening that would boost my spirit and I needed that. I opened the conversation by telling my family they needed to get their personal things out of my house at Lake Hubert.

Almost in unison, I heard, "Why?" I told them that I was planning to move and that brought another round of "whys" to which I responded I was so lonely living alone and concerned about what I would do if I got sick.

The next question was, "Where would you go?" My reply was, "I don't know, but it won't be in the Twin Cities because I've already done that." There was a pause. Then Florraine, who was working in the kitchen, must have overheard this because, she stepped into the room and said directly to me, "How about Northfield?" In just a few seconds I said, "BINGO!" I had not thought of moving to Northfield, but it made a lot of sense! It would be convenient for most of my family and it is not far from my hometown of Cannon Falls. I already knew Northfield, having attended St. Olaf College for two years. St. Olaf also offers much good musical entertainment through the colleges.

Starting Over in Northfield

In January, I started looking at housing options in Northfield. With help from Elizabeth, Florraine, my sister Marilyn and her husband, Ken, I found a new townhouse in the pre-sheetrock stage. By making a few changes, I could have a woodworking shop, an electrical shop, a large family room, a second bedroom and bath, and a large storeroom in the well-lit lower level. The house is next door to Bethel Lutheran Church and only a half-mile from St. Olaf College where I met Lorraine in 1946. It's also part of the Northfield Retirement Community that includes assisted living and long-term care facilities – just the right place for me to be at this stage of my life.

Before I moved in on May 3, 2007, I walked over to Bethel Lutheran Church and met the pastor. When he found out about my background, he said, "Jerry, we have a dreadful sound system." When he showed it to me, I had to agree.

The people at Bethel Church welcomed me with open arms. I enhanced the sanctuary audio system and finished a four-camera television production facility, so our services could be broadcast on Northfield's channel 12 several times each week. As a result, new families joined Bethel after seeing our services on TV. I designed and built four new audio-visual systems in the $4.5-million addition to the church facility. It was a very rewarding experience and helped to fill the void in my life after losing Lorraine. I also sang in the Bethel adult choir under the direction of Dan Kallman and with the Northfield Troubadours, a 35-voice old men's chorus.

When I met John Severson, a retired pastor at the UCC church in Northfield that needed help with their sound system, I found a real soulmate. He had two Volvos that he picked up in Sweden, sells Mac computers at the Apple Store in the Mall of America, and evaluates Tom-Tom GPS units. Together we restructured the sound system at his church.

In May 2007, my brother Keith, who lost his wife, Pauline, a year after Lorraine died, realized a life-long dream when we traveled together to Sweden. We began by picking up a new

Jerry and Keith go to Sweden

Volvo S-80 sedan at the factory in Gothenburg. Keith drove while I navigated. It was a thrill to visit the birthplaces of three of our grandparents. We would have visited the fourth but ran out of time. It was the trip of a lifetime. We were hosted by four gracious families of cousins with whom I had corresponded by email for years but never met face to face. They were superb tour guides and helped immensely with our lack of Swedish. One of the ladies found living relatives in two of our ancestral lines which opened the door to new genealogical information for us. We gained much better insight into why our grandparents emigrated from Sweden. Keith, who was politically conservative, declared that Sweden was "not bad for a socialist country."

Starting Over with Florraine

At this point, I had two companions in my life. One was Fancie, my six-year-old miniature black poodle who had lost nearly all her vision. She and I took mile-long walks twice a day, so we were literally the slow leading the blind. My other companion was Lorraine's identical twin sister, Florraine, whose 91-year-old husband, Bill, was failing rapidly and seldom recognized her when she visited him. Because she lived only thirty minutes away, we were able to attend social gatherings, entertainment events and family gatherings together — so much more enjoyable than attending alone.

Florraine's husband, Bill, died on January 12th from severe injuries suffered when he fell a few months earlier. Since we were both 82 years old, Florraine and I decided not to wait too long, so on June 6, 2009, we were married at Bethel Lutheran Church.

Our wedding was a small family affair with forty guests, nearly all family members. The music and the scripture readings were done by our talented kids and grandkids.

Jerry and Florraine on their wedding day

Jody Hoffman, Florraine's daughter, was matron of honor and my son, Paul was my best man. The reception was in the new Christian Life Center of the church. Our pastor had been seriously injured in a terrible fall off Barn Bluff in Red Wing just a week before the wedding, but we were blessed to have a youthful retired Bethel pastor, Clark Cary, perform the ceremony for us. Considering our years of familiarity, he excused Florraine and me from the usual pre-marital counseling sessions.

A week later we drove to Ashville, North Carolina, for the wedding of Florraine's grandson, Alex Trygstad. That was not our honeymoon, although it was a beautiful drive and wedding. Moving Florraine's household furnishings into my already crowded house was quite a task. We gave away as much as possible to family members and then had a garage sale at her former home in Hastings. The rest was donated to the Senior's Used-A-Bit shop in Northfield. We installed a lot of wall cabinets in my garage for things too good to throw out (yet). We also increased the capacity of our bedroom closet, with help from Ikea, to accommodate Florraine's wardrobe.

In February 2010, we took our delayed honeymoon trip to Kihei, Maui. Unfortunately, we chose a bad week – the week of the Chilean tsunami. It was so cold and windy that we couldn't walk the beach comfortably.

I was asked to design and install a sound system in the one-hundred-fifty-year old Valley Grove Church, near Nerstrand – a truly special building situated on a rural high-wooded hill. It still has an operational tracker pipe organ bought in 1911. While it was a very basic sound system, it was one of the most enjoyable jobs I have ever done. The congregation had disbanded in 1973 because of the close proximity of other Lutheran churches, but in recent years, it has become a favorite place for summer weddings. The new system permits grandparents to hear the service.

As soon as that job had been completed, the staff at Bethel Church asked me to install two sixty-five-inch television screens in the chancel. In the process, we discovered the north wall of the sound room enclosed an empty area that measured twelve feet by four feet. That space gave us room to expand the audio and video capabilities for weekday and Sunday activities.

Traveling the World and Making Trips to the ER

Florraine and I became enthusiastic travelers, something not possible with our previous spouses because of their health issues. In May, we enjoyed a ten-day trip with Trafalgar Tours to the Canyon Country in Arizona and Utah, even visiting the Grand Canyon during a snowstorm. From there, we traveled to Zion and Bryce National Parks and saw spectacularly colorful rock formations. Neither of us had seen the canyons before. We met many interesting travel companions and flew home from Las Vegas without a single casino visit.

We looked for opportunities to travel to places where neither of us had ever been. In July 2011 we took an ocean cruise – a first for both of us – aboard the SS *Zaandam* to Alaska. We boarded at Vancouver, Canada, and made stops at Ketchikan, Juneau, Skagway, and Seward. The shore excursions brought us into contact with the natives so we could learn about their way of life. The weather was unusually fine, and the natives said we were greatly blessed. We agreed.

At Seward, we boarded to a bus to Anchorage, and then enjoyed a ride on a restored historic train for our scenic trip to Denali National Park for a few days of guided exploration of this immense park the size of Connecticut. That visit gave us a deep appreciation for the immensity of Alaska. We added a flight around Mt. McKinley because the peak was invisible from the ground that day. The historic train continued on to Fairbanks. Other highlights were a paddle-wheel boat to a native Alaskan village, and we visited with the family of Susan Butcher, the four-time winner of the Iditarod sled dog race.

During our Alaskan cruise, we signed up for a fourteen-day Baltic Sea cruise in July of 2012, but it was not to be. In February, Florraine woke up with her left leg numb and cold. Our family doctor diagnosed the problem as near total blockage in the left leg artery and immediately sent us to Mayo Clinic where the surgeon removed the 98 percent blockage and sent us home the next day. At a follow-up visit in April, the Mayo doc said, "Cruise!"

Then on May 2nd, Florraine woke me up thinking she was having another heart attack. A 911 call brought the ambulance to our door and Florraine to the ER. The diagnosis was just indigestion. Whew! Maybe we could still go on the cruise. But on June 1st, Florraine was very nauseated at breakfast. After some quick tests at the Northfield hospital, she was diagnosed with atrial fibrillation with her heart beating more than 200 times per minute. An IV medication brought her heartbeat down to near normal in a few seconds, but she was kept in the hospital for a week while they adjusted the dosage. The discharge doctor said, "Take the cruise, it will do her good!"

Great! However, on June 13th, she asked for help to get out of bed. When I tried she screamed with excruciating pain in her low back. My only option was to call 911. After another ambulance trip to the ER and several days in the hospital, the pain was largely gone, but undiagnosed so they discharged her. I asked the doc if it could have been a muscle spasm and he said, "Quite possibly." A quick visit to our chiropractor and a massage therapist cleared up the pain. We could still go on the cruise!

In July we were at the Northfield Hospital for a pre-cruise checkup with her Mayo cardiologist. After listening to her heart, he exclaimed, "Cancel your cruise. She needs a pacemaker as soon as we can schedule it." He set up a consultation for July 17th. The pacemaker was implanted the next day and a day later we drove home. The change in Florraine was dramatic.

She had color in her face and newfound energy, but, it was too late for the cruise.

Florraine was happy to be cooking again. In mid-August she prepared a full dinner, but in turning from the stove she lost her balance and fell, hitting her right arm on an open drawer. I came running and found her on the floor holding her arm but dared not lift her because her arm was broken and bleeding badly. Another 911 call, another ambulance ride, and another ER visit where the doctor on call sewed up the wound, set her arm with a temporary splint, and hospitalized her. On Thursday, the orthopedic doc saw her between scheduled surgeries and reset it using fluoroscopy. She was able to go home the following day, Friday, August 17th in time for a homeowner's association party on our patio.

I realized we had forgotten her discharge medications at the hospital and went to fetch them. I left her resting comfortably in a recliner, but when I returned home less than 15 minutes later, she was on the floor with her arm re-broken! "What happened?" "I'm sorry," Florraine replied. "I dropped my can of pop and went to pick it up." Another 911 call and ambulance ride to the ER: she was hospitalized for three more days. On August 29th the orthopedist inserted a metal rod to reconnect the bones in her arm and she was discharged the next day.

Now we realized I could not physically handle her if she fell again so we agreed she needed to recover at the Northfield Care Center within walking distance of our house. I walked over at noon and dinner times to feed her because it was awkward for her to feed herself with her right arm in a splint.

The physical therapists at the Care Center recommended physical and occupational therapy at the Center for Sports Medicine and Rehabilitation in Northfield after her release. CSMR is in the same building as the orthopedic doctor's office.

On September 27th, following one of our rehab visits, Florraine lost her balance just a few feet from our car and fell flat on her face on the sidewalk. She broke her glasses and wounded her face and arms. Because she was now on a blood thinner there was blood all over the place. Within a minute medical staff came with a wheelchair and wet towels. Ironically, there were no doctors there that day so once again we drove to see our friends at the ER.

In January, we drove south on Highway 52 to the Mayo Clinic's Imbalance Lab to learn why both of us fall. Florraine's cause was a bad hip replacement installed in 2000, but because of her age, the doctors were reluctant to re-operate. I was diagnosed with normal pressure hydrocephalus (water on my brain.) A Mayo neurologist was not convinced of that diagnosis, instead thinking I had spinal stenosis. After three months and three MRI scans, each lasting an hour, he apologized for being wrong, but he didn't know what I had. I found an experienced neurosurgeon in St. Paul who installed a stent to relieve the pressure in my brain. The recovery was slow, painful, and complicated; we learned to get the pressure set right by trial and error.

Back at Mayo it was discovered I had an undetected sinus infection that had been masked by the brain pain. By the time I got that cleared up, I had lost most of my hearing. The Lord took advantage of the situation to use me to invent a better-performing, lower-cost hearing aid.

Florraine drove me to a neurology appointment in St. Paul. As we walked to the medical building she lost her balance and fell flat on her face. She was a bloody mess, so we went to the ER. They wanted to hospitalize her, but she insisted on going to the hospital in Northfield for observation where she was released a few days later.

In 2014 we were able to enjoy a twelve-day motor coach tour visiting all of the New England states. Two busses travelled together, each with 54 passengers, a driver and a guide. On the way east we stopped at the Ford Museum and Niagara Falls. We anticipated seeing the famous fall colors of New England, but it turned out that the leaf colors were better in Minnesota that year. Regardless, we had an enjoyable and educational time seeing the famous Revolutionary War sites, including the sailing vessel, Constitution, Plymouth Rock, and the historic battle sites of Lexington and Concord.

In January and February of 2015, we took a fifteen-day Holland America cruise through the Panama Canal. It made a nice break from the coldest part of our Minnesota winter. The trip was awesome. We both lost about five pounds because our stateroom was at the ship's bow, and the three dining rooms were at the stern – a 750-foot stroll away. Making the round trip, three times a day was a lot of walking for us but with the outside temperature at 85 degrees, it was quite enjoyable. We flew to Fort Lauderdale to board the ship and flew home from San Diego. Florraine had minor heart surgery at the Mayo Clinic to clean out a blockage in an artery and put in a stent. She was sent home the next day with orders for thirty-six heart rehab appointments. Because that therapy was not available in Northfield, we chose to go to the new Mayo Health System Hospital in Cannon Falls – a 25-minute drive from our home.

Meeting Swedish cousins in Stockholm

In the spring of 2016, I received a letter from a 90-year old Swedish gentleman named Sven Brise. He was working on his genealogy records and wanted to learn what happened to one of his great-grandfather's brothers who had emigrated from Sweden for America in 1869. Sven enlisted help from a mutual relative in Sweden, Berit Jonsson, who knew the answer and gave Sven our addresses for the details.

In May, Florraine and I took our third cruise with Holland America, this time on the Baltic Sea. By the third day we agreed it would be our last cruise because pushing Florraine on her convertible walker was almost impossible on the ship's plush carpeting. Pushing her over the old cobblestone streets was simply intolerable. But I lost ten pounds in the process, so some good came of it.

The best part of that cruise was the six-hour layover in Stockholm. Before leaving home I emailed Sven, who lives in a suburb of Stockholm, to see if we could meet face to face. Sven replied it would take an earthquake to keep him away. His daughter, Eva, met us at the ship. We had a delightful lunch with them at the king's palace. Sven had invited seven other cousins whom I already knew from previous visits and correspondence.

Back in Northfield, on the evening of Tuesday, December 20, 2016, Florraine and I had supper as usual at the Parkview West dining room. The meal was a bit off and as the evening wore on, I felt very tired and crawled into bed early. In a short time, I made several trips to the bathroom to give up my supper. Feeling progressively worse, I called 911. The responders took me to the Northfield emergency room where I was diagnosed as having Norovirus and admitted as a patient. Two days later I was discharged, but Florraine arrived at the hospital with Norovirus and was put in the same bed I had just left. It was a sorry Christmas with her there and me at home alone. We celebrated Florraine's 90th birthday on December 29th quietly at home, not wanting to expose any family members to our germs.

A few weeks later, I was sitting next to Florraine in her bed and noticed her breathing was very irregular. I checked my watch and saw that her breaths were a minute apart. I thought "sleep apnea" so I made an appointment for her to see an ENT specialist that visits our Northfield clinic. Her sleep study indicated she indeed had central apnea, a conflict between the brain and heart. The doc said, "I just have two words for you, Jerry: Mayo Clinic."

The head of the sleep clinic at Mayo loaned us a recording oximeter with instructions to connect it to her finger at bedtime. If she got up at night I was to get up as well, record why she got up and for how long, and return the oximeter the next morning before 10 AM. By noon the next day, he called me and said she needed oxygen. That afternoon a company in St. Paul delivered an oxygen concentrator that extracts oxygen from the air – no tank!

Before this, Florraine went back to bed for a nap after breakfast until noon, followed by another nap after lunch until supper. After using the concentrator that first night, she was up at 7:30 and made breakfast. She was a changed person. But Florraine had more ambulance trips to the ER after falling three times. Altogether she had two thirty-day recovery stays in the Northfield Care Center.

As for me, I still take no prescription medications. I credit the genes provided by my Swedish grandparents for my good health. I celebrated my 90th on the 4th of July 2017, at granddaughter Svea Merry's country home near Rochester.

In 2018 Florraine had many ambulance trips to the emergency room including five rides in the month of November, usually the result of falls and usually at night. On November 12, she woke up about 3 AM, lost control of her walker and fell, striking her head against the wall. I called 911. The emergency crew arrived within 10 minutes. Tests showed that she had a brain bleed that could not be stopped, so she was released to come home the next day. That fall was the beginning of the end.

After a few days, because she had lost consciousness, I was advised to place Florraine in a hospice facility to keep her comfortable. She slipped away peacefully on the evening of November 17th. We rejoice in the knowledge that she has been reunited in heaven with her twin, Lorraine. They have a lot to talk about! I received so much support from the community, but especially from my three daughters, Susan and Elizabeth, and Florraine's daughter, Jody, my "third daughter." She reminds me I am her third dad.

Because of her love of books, it was suggested that memorial gifts for Florraine go to the Bethel church library, the Northfield Retirement Community Parkview West library where she borrowed several books every week, or to Luther Seminary where we had a lot of friends. The many monetary gifts received were passed along to those organizations.

From Florraine's memorial folder

Florraine Flora Williams was born December 29, 1926, in St. James, Minnesota, to Christian and Emmy (Schaper) Hoffman. She was raised in St. James, confirmed at First Lutheran Church, and in 1944, graduated from St. James High School. She attended St. Olaf College, graduating in 1948 with a bachelor's degree in Home Economics. She taught high school in Richfield, and after retirement continued to educate by volunteer tutoring in Minneapolis.

On June 11, 1950, Florraine married Joseph Wangen at First Lutheran Church in St. James in a double wedding with her twin sister, Lorraine. Joseph passed away unexpectedly on November 24, 1958, while the family lived in Oslo, Norway. On June 12, 1961, Florraine married Dr. William Trygstad in Minneapolis. Bill passed away on January 12, 2009. She married Jerry Williams (her twin sister's surviving husband) on June 6, 2009, at Bethel Lutheran Church and the couple made their home in Northfield.

Florraine was a woman of quiet dignity and strength. Never one to be outspoken, she would share that strength and her words of wisdom with her family when she thought necessary. Her faith was deep, and her answer to troubling questions was, "I'll pray about it and you should too." She traveled often to see members of the family who were ill or elderly to bring them her love and her delicious cooking. Her secret pleasure was clothes, and she enjoyed a good shopping trip. Florraine loved her family, was an avid reader, and did beautiful needlework.

Survivors include her husband, Jerry; son, Marcus (Robin) Trygstad of Houston, Texas; daughters Jody (Larry) Hoffman of Hastings, Minnesota, and Kirsti Trygstad of Sparta, Wisconsin; grandchildren Hillary, Kristina, Grant, Alexander, and Matthew; great-grandsons, Anders and Jonathan; and numerous loving nieces, nephews, and their families. She was preceded in death by her husbands, Joseph and William, grandson David, her identical twin Lorraine Williams, and her brother Waldo Hoffman. Florraine passed away at the age of 91 on Saturday evening, November 17, 2018, at Reflections on the Three Links campus in Northfield.

Starting Over – Yet Again

Florraine and I were blessed to live less than a mile from St. Olaf College where we could attend musical events. We only needed to drive up "The Hill." No tickets were needed except for the incomparable Christmas Festival.

I can look out my back windows to see Bethel Lutheran Church. My life in Northfield is filled by daily contact with well-educated, charming seniors, many of whom are Oles (St. Olaf grads, like me) who tell great stories. As a result, I have wonderful friendships. I am able to use the NRC facilities, including the dining room, so I continue go there for dinner, almost nightly instead of cooking at home. I am only an hour's drive away from my children and their families, except for the Beckmans who moved to State College, Pennsylvania.

It is so lonely to be living alone after having two wonderful wives. I am truly blessed to have my little dog Oliver with me. I got him in 2018 when Florraine gave me a Christmas card with the note, "Your gift is to get a dog."

One morning in the fall of 2019, after my morning Bible time, I said a prayer. "Lord, I was counting on having Florraine with me for another four, five, or six years, but you took her!

Florraine, Jerry and Oliver

I was astounded to hear him speak directly and clearly to me inside my head. He said, "Yes, Jerry, I took her because she was taking up too much of your time. You were chasing to the doctor, the hospital and the emergency room all the time, but she was not going to get any better, so I took her. Now she is having a great time getting re-acquainted with her sister. I am taking care of them, so don't worry about them. I'm caring for them. But now, Jerry, get busy and finish writing your book!" I could hardly believe what I had just heard. The Lord spoke to me! And He knows about my book! Wow!

Three days before Christmas in 2019 I got a call from my daughter, Susan. She must have sensed something wasn't right with me because she called her sister, Elizabeth, and asked her to drive down to my house to check on me. When Elizabeth and her husband, Roger, arrived, she put her hand to my forehead and said, "Dad, you're really sick. We're going to the hospital." We were in the emergency room by 8 PM. A battery of tests yielded no diagnosis. At 2 AM the doctor suggested they run still some more tests, but I said, "No way. I've got a radio interview in the morning. I'll come back after that." Liz and Roger brought me back home and made arrangements for my radio host to pick me up in the morning so I wouldn't have to drive myself.

The radio interview at KYMN was for the "Wayne Eddy Affair." This was my third interview with Wayne to tell some of my life stories – the stories you've been reading. As soon as I was finished, Liz and Roger whisked me back to the hospital where more tests were ordered. This time, the chest x-ray showed I had pneumonia and I was admitted.

Our family had planned to spend Christmas Day together at my house, so I was sad to spend Christmas Eve and Christmas Day in a hospital bed instead. But the kids and grandkids gathered at my house as planned and took turns visiting me. Even my dog Oliver, who was being cared for by my daughter Susan, came to see me. We were both ecstatic with this reunion. Oliver slept on my lap for at least two hours before they took him back.

Starting Over in a New Home

It took me awhile to get back up to speed after I got out of the hospital. I guess I didn't really make it all the way back, because my three kids all thought I might be better off living at Parkview West. For several years I had been having my dinner there every night, so I already had many friends and I had been terribly lonely after Florraine died.

On March 2nd, Elizabeth and I looked at an independent living apartment that was available in Parkview West. It has a living/dining room, one bedroom, and a wood-paneled room with lots of windows they called an enclosed porch – perfect to be my office. My family doctor supplied a document saying Oliver is my emotional support animal, so by law, this no-pets building had to allow him to live with me.

This was not a change I was enthusiastic about, but it made sense. After all, one reason I chose to live on the Northfield Retirement Community campus thirteen years earlier was so I could transition to the different levels of care if needed. The kids came to help me pack the things I would take with me, and on Tuesday, March 10th, my kids and a couple of strong men with a truck came to move my furniture – and my life – into unit 1215 at Parkview West on the Northfield Retirement Community campus.

By that evening most of my things were unpacked and put away, but Oliver and I both felt very much out of place. Everything except dinner in the dining room was unfamiliar. My kids returned a few times during the week to continue unpacking boxes of books and files, but then COVID-19 changed everything.

Chapter 12

THE CORONAVIRUS PANDEMIC CHANGED EVERYTHING

In the United States, we first became aware of the highly contagious coronavirus, known as COVID-19, (officially known as SARS-COV-2) in late January/early February 2020. It is believed the virus originated in a market in Wuhan, China, where wild animals are killed and sold as food for human consumption. The epidemic quickly grew into a world-wide pandemic. Despite restricting airline flights from China, the virus reached the U.S. and quickly spread across the country.

On March 7, 2020, Tim Walz, the governor of Minnesota, imposed a shelter-at-home rule, which closed all but essential businesses, including restaurants and most stores. Schools and colleges were also closed at that time.

People were told to wear face masks, stay at least six feet apart from others, and wash their hands frequently to avoid catching and spreading this terrible disease.

As I write about this in September 2020, more than 190,000 Americans have already died from the virus. At first it appeared to be most deadly for the elderly folks and people with pre-existing health issues, but it is apparent that people of any age can get it. Some will hardly notice while others sicken quickly and die.

My adult children, Elizabeth, Susan, and Paul, were concerned about me living alone. I had already decided to stop driving and sell my car. Collectively, they decided that I should sell my house and move into an assisted living building.

Florraine and I had routinely eaten our evening meals in the dining room at Parkview West, part of the Northfield Retirement Community just down the block from our house. It seemed logical to my children that I should move there because I already had a circle of friends.

Liz contacted the residence director and learned they had a one-bedroom-plus-den apartment I could rent. The kids packed the things I would need in my new apartment, and on March 10th a moving truck pulled into my driveway. However, exactly one week later the COVID-19 shelter-in-place order came and the building went on complete "lock-down" so visitors were no longer permitted to enter. My adult children could not help me finish getting settled in and organized.

The shut-down also meant the building's communal dining room was closed, so meals had to be delivered to my apartment on disposable Styrofoam dishes. One of the main reasons I had been willing to move into Parkview was to continue enjoying dinner with my friends. Now residents were discouraged from congregating anywhere, and if we did leave our apartments we were required to wear face-masks, and to keep a six-foot distance between us. Life became very lonely for everyone.

As my children worked to prepare my former house for sale, the only way they could deliver items I wanted was to push a button in the vestibule at Parkview's front entrance. A masked and gloved aide would come to the door, take whatever they brought, and carry it to my apartment.

Not long after moving into Parkview, it became apparent to me that I could no longer care for my little poodle, Oliver, the way I wanted and needed to do. So I did what was best for him and gave him to Cynthia Neubecker, a lady I met some months earlier when I was out walking with Oliver.

At that first meeting Cynthia got down on her hands and knees and started petting Oliver. He responded by licking her face! I could tell immediately that Cynthia was a real dog lover. We chatted for a few minutes and I learned that she was one of Elizabeth's former genealogy students. Her own little dog died only a few months earlier, so when Liz and I asked if she could take care of Oliver during moving day in March, she immediately said yes. When I later asked if she could take Oliver permanently she all but grabbed him. Oliver was very happy under her care. One of the highlights of my day was when they visited my office window during their daily walk. Cynthia and her sister were very kind to supply me with their handmade face masks.

My granddaughter Sarah also kept busy during the awful stay-at-home time by sewing high quality face masks and mailing them to people all over the country in ex-

Sarah (Wall) Beckman

161

change for a $25 donation to a charity of the recipient's choice. This has been her wonderful ministry from home – keeping people safe and encouraging charity at the same time. I am so proud of Sarah. She sent one of her beautifully made masks to me – dark gray with a small blue and yellow Swedish flag embroidered on it.

This is a good place to interrupt my story so a proud grandfather can tell you about his amazing granddaughter. When Sarah entered grade school, she had difficulty learning to read. Her problem was diagnosed as dyslexia. Fortunately, her family lived in Rochester, Minnesota, where The Reading Center specializes in helping children with dyslexia. With their help, Sarah overcame her challenge and went on to graduate from college with honors.

To minimize the chances of bringing the highly contagious virus into Parkview, the staff didn't want us to leave the building. So, my telephone and my window were my only connections to the outside world. I had frequent phone conversations with my kids. When they were in Northfield we sometimes chatted through the window. My son, Paul, brought over one of the bird feeders from my house and installed it on a pole outside my window. Cynthia made sure it always has seed in it. It brought me such pleasure to watch the birds.

My daughter, Elizabeth, got an application on her computer that allows her to access my computer, so whenever I had a computer problem, I'd just call Liz for help. I could watch her move my cursor across the screen and soon my problem would be fixed. Electronics have come a long way during my lifetime! Being able to see my family members, including grandchildren with Facetime and Zoom seems miraculous and it helps all of us cope with the isolation.

One day while Liz was visiting, she asked if I would like some help keeping track of my bills and writing the payment checks. I happily accepted her offer because in the move, I had lost my checkbook and was delinquent in my payments. In just a few days, Liz had it all under control and I was able to relax having been relieved of a job I had been doing for many years.

I was very unhappy living at Parkview. The staff members were not interested in making my life more enjoyable. It seemed that their typical response was, "No! You can't do that!" Elizabeth was making frequent trips to Northfield to deliver things to me and help with selling my house – a one-hundred-twenty-mile round trip. I recalled that before I was moved into Parkview, she made an attempt to get me into Waverly Gardens, senior housing very close to her home, but there were no openings. I asked her to try again. She was told they had one opening but another couple had the first right of refusal. I thought this called for prayer so, I asked the Lord to help that couple find a better place for them! Then Liz got a call that I could have the open apartment because the couple decided to stay in their home. Thank you, God.

On June 25th I moved into a one-bedroom-with-den apartment in The Arbor at Waverly Gardens in North Oaks, just a ten-minute drive from Liz's house. My apartment is much nicer than the one I had at Parkview. The staff is wonderful, and even the food is better and served on real dishes. Best yet, because The Arbor is a self-contained unit, the residents do not have isolate in their apartments and are free to enjoy the entire floor, including an outdoor patio, without wearing masks. My children have been able to get occasional passes to visit me in my apartment, and I can enjoy other visitors in the beautiful outdoor courtyard. It didn't take long for me to feel at home here.

The corona virus has changed everything. How much longer will we have to be separated from family and friends? I want to be able to hug my kids and grandkids. I miss going to church.

Please, dear Lord, rescue us from this plague. Amen.

Chapter 13

BITS & PIECES

MY SEVERAL NAMES

Written as an Elder Collegium class assignment in April 2012

Gerald was the name given me at my baptism, but when I was in the first grade and learning to print my name, my teacher, Miss Madsen, said, "Perhaps you would prefer to learn to print Jerry, because that is your nickname. That would be easier. All your classmates call you Jerry." Then she said, "Even though your real name Gerald begins with G, your nickname, Jerry, will begin with a J, because girls spell it with a G. Who would argue with their first grade teacher? They know everything!

I think that my father's unmarried sister, Olga, who was one of my baptismal sponsors, suggested the name "Gerald" to my parents because she always called me Gerald. When anyone asks me which name I prefer, I say, "Jerry, because it is only the IRS and that one aunt that calls me Gerald."

Ivar, my middle name, was given to me in honor of Dr. Ivar Sohlberg, M.D. He was the physician that my father interned under at Bethesda Hospital in St. Paul. He was also the doctor who delivered me on July 4th, 1927. He was also a member of First Lutheran Church in St. Paul, the church that my four grandparents attended. Ivar is a common Swedish given name. I have relatives in my family tree with that name. It is pronounced with a soft "I".

"GI" was the name that I was frequently called in the Navy because many service men at that time were identified by our first two initials. GI seemed to catch on later at Univac because it was short. It also seemed appropriate because during World War II those of us serving in the military were dubbed GI's, referring to the term for everything we wore was "Government Issue".

"giwill" is the name I use in my email address. That idea came to me because during the period from 1955 to 1958, I was involved in the design of the Univac File Computer. Four of us engineers were specifically recruited from other project teams to design this computer. It was to be the first commercial computer to be built in St. Paul for Remington Rand and it was a crash project because the company desperately needed a computer to compete with a newly announced IBM business computer.

Initially, the design team met almost daily to review our progress. Ironically, the four engineers on this project all had last names that began with "W." I was responsible for the memory section of the machine. When there was a question about who would do this or that, Jim Wright would always pipe up with, "GI will!"

"Papa Jerry" is the name my oldest daughter came up with when her first child was started to talk. Her other grandfather became Papa Jim. Both he and I liked the names. They stick today for both of us now that those grandchildren have children. I shorten it in my emails to PJ.

"Grampa" is the name that my daughter, Susan's children

call me, but I forget that at times in my communication with them and flip to Papa Jerry.

∞

AN INFLUENTIAL PERSON IN MY LIFE:
MY UNCLE ALFER STROM

Written as an Elder Collegium class assignment in April 2012

He was always Uncle Al to me. He was my mother's brother. His parents were Swedish immigrants. My Grandfather Strom left his home in Sweden in 1888 when he was twenty years old. My Grandmother Strom left Sweden in 1889 when she was just eighteen years old. They both came to America by themselves. He left to find better opportunities. She left because she felt abused and unloved at home, being forced to work barefoot in cold muddy fields.

On a rainy night, they met at a Luther League gathering at First Lutheran Church in St. Paul, Minnesota. Afterward, they shared an umbrella while walking to the streetcar stop near the church. That must have been a magical night because they were married in 1894, five years after arriving in St. Paul. At that time, both were living with Swedish families that had immigrated before them.

My Uncle Al was their first-born, born at 355 Mississippi Street in St. Paul on March 13, 1895. My mother was born four years later, sandwiched in between two more brothers.

Uncle Al was one of my baptismal sponsors. My aunt, Olga Williams, was the other. He took that responsibility seriously, always sending me a birthday card with a scripture reference penned inside. I was baptized at Bethesda Hospital the day after I was born because the doctors did not expect me to survive. Eighty-five years later, I can say with certainty the doctors were wrong! I wondered if Uncle Al watched over me so faithfully for many years because my mother, who was his only living sister, died just before my seventh birthday, and he felt a responsibility to her to see to it that I, too, would become a man of God.

Al, as a child, was eager to learn to read, write and speak English, even though Swedish was spoken at home. As soon as he finished the eighth grade of public school, he was told that he needed to get a job to help support the family. He worked on the railroad for a time before finding a job at R. L. Polk & Company as an office boy, then as a proofreader, compiler, enumerator and bill collector.

He desired to add to his education since he was denied the opportunity to attend high school, so he enrolled in night school. We don't know which one.

Upon graduation from night school, he enrolled at the University of Minnesota in the business school majoring in accounting. To support his family during that period, he got a job at the St. Paul Post Office as a temporary worker filling in for absentees. Because the temporaries did not get paid unless they worked, he got up early to be first in line from those being selected to work. In that job, he earned a variety of skills by not always working in the same area.

At age twenty-two, he married Ellen Marie Nelson whom he met at First Lutheran. A son, Robert, was born in their first year followed by a daughter, Evelyn Marie. Robert became an FBI Agent working in Tennessee. Evelyn became the wife of a Lutheran pastor serving Lutheran parishes in Seattle Washington, Cambridge and Willmar, Minnesota, Buffalo, New York, and Atlanta, Georgia.

Evelyn recalls her father doing his homework on one side of the kitchen table while she and Robert studied on the other side. While working as a temporary, he became aware of a full-time job opening that required taking the postal department's civil service exam. With his university diploma and his accounting skills, he was well qualified for the job of Postal Inspector, auditing the outstate post offices. He placed eleventh out of the 700 who took the exam.

The Postal Inspector's job placed him initially in Minnesota and later in other states. When my father remarried in 1936, following my mother's death in 1934, my brother Keith and I lived with the Strom family in Mankato for two weeks during my parents' honeymoon. That was a special time for us with many memories.

When their children were in grade school the Strom family moved to Kentucky to be near the area where he was working. He traveled that area by train but always tried to be home for the weekends.

When it came time for Robert and Evelyn to start high school, they moved back to Minnesota. Both Robert and Evelyn graduated from Minnehaha Academy and Gustavus Adolphus College.

Uncle Al was recognized for his detailed reports and dedication to the work and was moved to Washington D.C to serve as an executive accountant, then as assistant to the controller. Then Postmaster General James A. Farley, himself an accountant by training, promoted him to Commissioner of Budget in 1945. That was the highest civil service job level.

Sadly, we children lost contact with all of the Strom family after my father remarried because my stepmother would not allow it. After I was married and Elizabeth was born, I decided to reconnect with the Stroms. We did that in time for Grandfather Strom to meet my wife, Lorraine and to learn that he was destined to have another great-grandchild. I have a picture of Grandmother Strom holding Elizabeth a few years later. As a genealogist, that picture is precious to Liz.

Lorraine and I visited Uncle Al and Aunt Helen in 1951 during our deferred honeymoon and had the privilege of seeing his impressive office in the Farley Building. We stayed with them for several days and were able to see much of the capitol.

When Al retired in 1954 from the postal department, as it was called at that time, he and Helen moved back to Minneapolis. He accepted a job with the Augustana Lutheran Church office as the treasurer of the Board of Foreign Missions. He also offered his services to Bethesda Hospital in St. Paul, working with the treasurer.

I was able to visit Al and Helen several times while they were living in Augustana Home. During one visit, Al mentioned that he was having difficulty hearing in the chapel. This was a great opportunity for me to in a small way repay him for his lovingkindnesses to me for so many years. I installed one of our Williams Sound assistive listening systems in the chapel and asked the chaplain that it be dedicated to Al and Helen.

I was also able to bring my father to visit Al on one of his infrequent visits to Minnesota. It was special to me to bring these two brothers-in-law together after many years of separation. Uncle Al was my idol as the kind of man I always wanted to be.

❧

LEO SLATTERY AND OUR POCKET WATCHES

When I was 86, going on 87 and doing my daily read of the newspaper obituaries, I saw one for Leo Slattery who had worked at Engineering Research (ERA) and Control Data at the same times as I did, though we never worked on the same projects. I believe Leo and I were the only ones at that company who carried pocket watches. It seems they were no longer fashionable and inconvenient compared to a wristwatch. Lorraine had to make watch pockets for me whenever I bought new pants, but she never complained.

I bought my pocket watch from a friend, Herman Madland. In fact, Herman bought our house in Roseville when he gave in to pressure from his father, a Lutheran pastor, to quit his job as a foundry superintendent in Mankato and enroll at Luther Seminary to also become a pastor. Herman and his wife needed to be closer to the "sem" at the same time we were moving to Edina to be closer to my new job at Transistor Electronics.

Herman's father-in-law was a Great Lakes ship captain. Whenever he was in port, the captain visited pawn shops to search out old watches. His hobby was collecting old watches and making them run again. Occasionally he sold them if he had duplicates.

I told Herman I would like to have a pocket watch someday, if it wasn't too expensive. A short time later, he came up with one I bought for forty dollars. It is a Ball railroad watch; they are extremely accurate.

Somehow, my friend Leo saw mine one day, and we compared watches. Ever after that, when we passed in the hallway, we stopped to compare the time. It was a fun ritual.

⚘

EARLY DIGITAL COMPUTER STANDARDS
AND
A GENTLEMAN NAMED JOHN RANKIN

I met John Rankin for the first time in 1975 when he worked for IBM. I would like to reconnect because meeting John was a life changing moment for both me and my wife, Lorraine. I would like to express my gratitude to him.

I had recently resigned from my position at Transistor Electronics, a company I helped to start, to return to work in the computer industry at Control Data Corp (CDC). The first job I accepted at Control Data was to create a new division to design and competitively manufacture components for the company's hardware divisions; items those divisions were procuring for use in their products but were unsatisfactory in terms of price or performance, or both.

It became apparent I could organize my new division around regulated DC power supplies for starters. The Power Supply Division succeeded so well at that goal that I got the attention of Dr. John Baird, CDC's VP of Research and Engineering who came to CDC from IBM. Dr. Baird came to my office to ask if I would accept a job on his staff overseeing the engineering departments of all the divisions. I accepted his flattering offer because I had already completed my initial goal at CDC with the formation of the CDC Power Supply Division.

After a few weeks in the new position, Dr. Baird thought my job title should be changed to General Manager of CDC Technical Standards. That title could be helpful because CDC's growth came about through the acquisition of a series of small companies. The company's growing pains were revealed at customer sites when products from different CDC divisions were assembled into large complex systems. Not only were the equipment cabinets painted different colors, the CDC instruction and maintenance manuals on the customers' shelves bore little or no resemblance to each other. Even worse, the electrical power and signal connectors to and from the equipment varied, so the customer engineers doing the system installation were on their own to sort out and retrofit those discrepancies.

These problems of non-standardization resulted in establishing a corporate engineering committee. The engineering managers of all of the divisions met to discuss and agree on technical standards for the company's hardware products. Eventually similar action was taken with the software operations.

Several people already in the company became members of my staff to document and publish the agreed-upon standards and introduce them to all the divisions. During this time, computers were rapidly becoming so commonplace in business, government, and industry that it became necessary for computers of by different manufacturers to communicate with each other. IBM led the way with this effort by up-dating an existing high-tech non-profit organization that was re-named the Computer and Business Equipment Manufacturers Association (CBEMA).

I persuaded the high-level management of CDC to join CBEMA so it could have a voice in setting the required technical standards for inter-computer communications. CDC management designated me as CDC's representative at CBEMA meetings. It was then my responsibility to identify the most-qualified CDC person to serve with an American National Standards Institute (ANSI) Working Group to produce American National Computer Standards to achieve compatibility for all computer users.

The first time I met with the American National Computer Standards Planning and Priorities Committee is a moment etched in my memory and is the reason for this story about John Rankin. When I walked in the room for the first meeting of the CBEMA Computer Standards Planning and Priorities Committee, a statesman-like gentleman rose to his feet and motioned for me to take the empty chair next to him. After the meeting was called to order by the acting leader, we were invited to rise, give our names and the names of our company affiliation. I introduced myself as Jerry Williams with Control Data Corp. My new friend introduced himself as John Rankin with IBM. All of the others did likewise.

The next order of business was to elect officers for our committee. The acting leader asked for nominations for the position of committee chair. Surprise! My new friend, John Rankin, stood up and nominated me for chair person, and I was elected unanimously. Then I learned the elected chair person was also to be America's representative to the International Computer Standards Committee. Wow! This meant meetings in London, Paris, Venice, and other equally wonderful places.

A visit to Montreaux, Switzerland, came about because CDC had a Series 6,000 computer system user-group named VIM for Roman numeral 6,000, that met in various cities around the world. Because of my awareness of new computer standards being created, Dr. Baird felt I should attend the VIM meetings to inform CDC computer-users of the opportunity they would have to participate in drafting the new standards. That international responsibility meant Lorraine and I would see even more of the world.

The following year, I was unanimously re-elected as chair of the CBEMA standards committee. I am grateful for the opportunity for world travel because of a gentleman named John Rankin. I have not heard from him in many years, but recently learned that he passed away in 2018 in Whanganui, New Zealand. I hope to share this story with his family if they can be located.

JERRY'S PATENTS

ADVICE FOR DESIGN ENGINEERS

The best kind of originality is that which comes after a sound apprenticeship; that which shall prove to be a blending of a firm conception of all useful precedent and progressive tendencies of an able mind. For let a man be as able and original as he may; he cannot afford to discard knowledge of what has gone before or is now going on in his own backyard.

– source unknown

Even if it is not in the books – try it. It might be in the cards.

– E. F. Mc Donald, Jr.,
President of Zenith Radio Corp

A consumer who dictates quality into a product by tightening of a specification alone has not only raised his own prices for a product of unchanged quality but has also paved the way for his own disaster by believing in a product improvement that does not exist.   – source unknown

There is hardly anything in the world that some man cannot make a little worse and sell little cheaper, and the people who consider price only are this man's lawful prey.

– John Ruskin

Change without cause is activity without progress.

– source unknown

OUR SPECIAL FAMILY VACATIONS (1958-1987)

A Month in Europe for Jerry & Lorraine

In the 1950s, Lorraine and I had many friends who had recently been to Europe. I had been working long hours creating Control Data's new Cedar Engineering Division which would design and build products for other CDC divisions having problems with outside suppliers. I needed a break.

So, in 1965 Lorraine and I decided to take a one-month pleasure trip to Europe to help rejuvenate me. The trip was a '"sampler" trip for us. We were interested in visiting many countries but couldn't decide which ones, so we chose to visit each for a few days. Then the next time in Europe we would stay longer in the ones we enjoyed the most and that was exactly what we did. We started our trip in the Netherlands to see the colorful tulip fields – a delightful experience. Then we visited Austria, Germany, Switzerland, Norway, Sweden and Denmark. They were all welcoming and had beautiful scenery. We met my father's cousins in Sweden and that began friendships that have only grown deeper to this day.

Colonial Williamsburg

This was one of our best vacation trips ever. Lorraine wanted very much to visit Williamsburg and decided that we should do it over the Christmas holiday when they do so much special decorating. She was spot on. It was a fabulous time to be there.

There were no crowds in spite of what a person might expect during the Christmas holiday.

Lorraine and I were upset with Elizabeth's attitude the first days. Finally, Lorraine confronted her and asked what her problem was. She said, "Well, who do these people here think they are? They believe this is where America began, but we are taught in school it began with the pilgrims settling at Plymouth Rock in Massachusetts!" With that we had the answer – our history books written from a northern-state perspective had created the confusion.

Greenfield Village and The Ford Museum

We arrived in the Detroit area after an enjoyable ferryboat ride across Lake Michigan. By taking the ferry, we shortened our drive a few hundred miles and had the use of our own car when we arrived. Greenfield Village is the location of Thomas Edison's Menlo Park Laboratory, the Wright brother's shop, and many other historic places that Henry Ford had gathered together. The Ford Museum is a massive collection of farm machinery, clothing, dishes etc. It was quickly apparent to Lorraine and me that she and our teen-aged girls were interested in seeing different things than Paul and me, so we decided to split and meet at the Dearborn Inn at the end of the day. Paul was perhaps about seven years old, so I told him that we would quit when he was tired of walking. Well, we quit when they were locking the doors at five o'clock. Today, Paul has no recollection of that experience. My daughter, Sue, a psychiatrist, told me that long-term memory does not develop until after age seven.

Kihei Beach Resort, Maui

In 1993, on impulse we bought a condominium apartment in Kihei, Maui. Hawaii. Previously, another Lake Hubert family who annually vacationed on Maui invited us to join them the following year because there was a two-week vacancy during the time they would be there. I had served in the Navy in Hawaii during the war and was a bit skeptical of the physical conditions of Hawaii after the war, but Lorraine really wanted to go.

We were not disappointed when we got there. Lorraine fell in love with the place. The second day we were there, I saw her reading in a lounge chair on the lawn about fifty feet from the ocean and she asked me to see if there were any vacancies for the same time next year. I was disappointed to hear there were none, so I asked if any of the units were ever for sale. I learned there were two currently available. Without much hesitation we chose a second-floor unit to minimize steps in that six-story building.

The individual condo owners jointly owned the building and managed the resort with a board of directors and front desk staff. Their annual board meeting was in mid-October. That was also when most repair and remodeling took place in the apartments.

In 1995 I was elected treasurer of the resort board because I could operate the newly purchased office computer and train the office ladies.

The unit we bought needed some modernizing. We found several local independent contractors on the recommendation of other owners and rebuilt the kitchen and both baths in the following two years. That made it nicer for our guests. We always visited the resort in February to escape Minnesota winters and again in mid-October for the repair projects and the owners meeting. We developed great friendships with the other owners. Most were from the west coast, because they could fly to Maui in just four hours.

We sold the unit in 2002 because Lorraine was having so much backpain she could no longer fly those long hours. It took quite a long time to sell because world-wide pilot shortages at that time restricted the number of long overseas flights, and that reduced the number of tourists. We brought Florraine along with us several times. Keith and Pauline Williams visited us, and we had a great time together showing them around the island. Elizabeth and her then husband, David Wall, used the condo with their kids. We were there in 1993, 1994, and 1995 for two extended periods.

In 2009, Florraine and I were married in Northfield and chose to celebrate our marriage with a one-week honeymoon on the island.

※

THE FIRST CLOCK I BUILT

As new members of Normandale Lutheran Church in 1958, Lorraine and I were invited to join a couples' group that met monthly in members' homes for Bible study. One of the first homes we visited was that of Rudy and Gert Westerberg. As we were finding a place to sit for the evening their grandfather clock struck the hour, followed by the familiar Westminster chime. Lorraine and I traded glances that said, "We should have one of those someday."

Rudy told me he built the clock case from a kit of pre-cut boards. After he finished assembling the case, he went back to the Kuempel Clock Shop and picked up the clock works he had pre-paid as part of the kit. It was easily installed and chimed beautifully.

Lorraine and I decided a grandfather clock would make our new living room seem more welcoming. We visited the Kuempel shop, staffed entirely by grandfathers. We selected a case design called The Spirit of '76 and chose cherry wood. We found it was a good choice because when it is cut or sanded, cherry releases a very pleasant fragrance. As I began to assemble the clock case, I discovered the pre-cut boards did not fit together well. Fortunately, my wood-working shop was well-equipped with hand and power tools.

When I returned to the Kuempel shop to pick up the works for my clock, I visited with Mr. Kuempel's daughter who had taken over the business after he passed away. She informed me her father's old-country method was to cut the boards slightly over-size and then file and sand the pieces until they fit together perfectly.

Once the case was complete, it was time to apply stain and a finish coat, something I had done many times for other projects. I searched for an oil stain that was a close match to our best furniture pieces, but when applied it looked blotchy. It took many hours of sanding to get down to the bare wood again. Eventually, I found a different type of stain of a comparable color and sampled it on surfaces that would not be visible. Once the stain was dry to the touch I lightly sanded all of the pieces back to a smooth surface.

To avoid the air-born dust that is inevitable in the home of an active family I decided to apply the finish coat in the bathroom. So, I took a day off from work and vacuumed the bathroom floor, walls, and ceiling, and wiped everything down with a damp sponge. After shutting the dog in one of the bedrooms, I stripped down to my underwear and tip-toed into the bathroom to apply the first coat of quick-drying finish to the case.

I left the bathroom long enough for the surface to be dry enough to apply a second coat. Just when the second coat was nearly dry, the bathroom door opened and my son Paul said, "What are you doing? I've looked all over the house for you!"

The next step in building the clock was to pick up and install the clock works in the case. What a thrill to hear the beautiful Westminster chime for the first time! That clock has provided many years of service since then. I later built two more grandfather clocks, one for my first grandchildren from my daughters, Liz and Sue. Those clocks were presented on the first birthdays of my grandchildren, Svea in 1977 and Christopher in 1982.

✑✖✎

My Guardian Angel

All through my life, I have had a feeling that someone or something was very close to me, watching over me. As I began writing this book and I needed to recall details of events that occurred in my life, I began to realize that someone or something had influenced my choices and decisions so that I made the best choices. Sometimes the result was not the one I expected or preferred to make, yet it proved to be the better one in the "long run."

When I reached my 90s, I became more interested in my Christian faith and read my Bible more attentively, looking for how and why answers in what I was reading. The result was that I developed an appetite for my Bible because I could see God is a gracious God and He gave us His Son to us for a reason. He gave us Jesus to guide and support us in our daily lives and to intercede for us with God, our creator.

Elizabeth, my first child became interested in the information I had collected about my four grandparents who emigrated from Sweden in the mid-1800s. In the course of her genealogy research Elizabeth uncovered the medical details of my mother's death, as follows:

My birth mother, Elmie Strom, died when I was only six years old, the result of a surgeon's mishap. As a result, she died from sepsis. Her medical record shows she lingered with a very high fever for three days before she passed away. Later in my life, I learned from her close friends that Elmie was an ardent prayer warrior, having taught Bible classes at the Lutheran Bible Institute and at our church in Cannon Falls.

One day while walking my dog, in my mind's eye I visualized her lying on her deathbed praying. I imagined that she was saying, "Lord, when I die, my children won't have a mother. Lord, you need to care for my three children. You have to take care of Jerry, Keith and little Marilyn. Lord, please promise me you will do that!"

Even in my limited understanding of how God works, I believe God heard my birth mother's plea and I think now that God appointed a guardian angel for each of us three children – one for me, her six-year-old-son, one for Keith, her three-year-old-son, and one for Marilyn, her 18 month-old-daughter. My brother and sister have told me they have had similar experiences.

Angel Stories

Here are just a few of the times my guardian angel has helped me recently.

Finding the lost Cannon Falls Mayo Hospital Dedication Check, December 17, 2015

On this day, that was also the last of forty heart therapy appointments that Florraine had at the new Cannon Falls Hospital, I had a check for $100,000 on my desk. It was the last of five payments to fulfill my $500,000 pledge to Mayo Clinic in exchange for the naming rights for an addition to the new hospital to memorialize my father.

The intent of the gift was to recognize my father's forty-four years of dedicated care for his patients in Cannon Falls. I felt strongly that he deserved some form of lasting public recognition. I called Bill Preist, the hospital administrator before leaving, to make certain he would be there to accept the check.

As we headed for the car, I went to my office to pick up the envelope with the check. I could not find it! I shared my panic with Florraine. She said, "Just sit down for a minute and relax and you'll find it." I did that and went back into the office. The envelope laid squarely in the middle of my desk. Thank you, Angel!

That was almost unbelievable! At that moment, I realized that God's angels are real and are caring for me personally. It was the first of many such incidents in store for me and they are still happening as I write this.

Finding Florraine's Hearing Aids, January 26, 2018

Florraine and I had returned home from some errands. We wanted to put in her hearing aids so she could hear me from the stove where I was making supper, but we could not find them. I turned the search over to my angels and started fixing a bowl of soup. Then, I heard an unexpected clang behind me and turned around to see the black hearing aid box on the counter next to the fridge! Thank you again, Angel!

Florraine's Hearing is Restored, March 27, 2018

Florraine's hearing had continued to deteriorate for several years. We had her ears cleaned by a very experienced ear, nose and throat doctor. We bought $6,000 hearing aids and $600 hearing aids and they helped bit, but she lost them regularly and I was at my wits end trying to find a good answer. As I pondered our options, I realized that we had not prayed for God's help, so we did. I took Florraine's hand and asked my/our angel to please restore Florraine's hearing, if possible. On this morning, when I woke up Florraine, I spoke to to her and she responded. Then I suddenly realized that she was hearing me unaided!

❦

THE NIGHT I ALMOST BOUGHT THE LAKE
JULY 7, 1996

My son, Paul, has a year-round lake home on Lake Sarah, near Rockford, Minnesota, about fifteen miles west of Minneapolis. He and his wife, Evone, enjoy their cozy home, built about 1950 by a European refugee couple. When they bought the house, they recognized it needed a lot of TLC to bring it up to their standards, but they were taking their time and trying to enjoy the lake during the process.

Paul bought a used runabout that he painstakingly restored before they were married. But he discovered that year that the plywood floor supporting the fiberglass hull was de-laminating, so they had no boat to use in those rare moments when they had a few minutes to enjoy the lake. They both wanted to buy another boat but could not decide which style of boat to get, so I offered to loan them our fourteen-foot aluminum fishing boat for the balance of the summer.

After celebrating my birthday on the 4th of July with us at Lake Hubert, Paula nd Evone stayed longer than our other kids' families. It was about seven o'clock that Sunday evening and dusk was approaching when I suggested we ought to get the boat out of the lake and onto the trailer before dark so they could be on their way home.

We connected my boat trailer to Paul's car, and I sent him to the public access landing on the west shore of our lake. I walked down to the dock and found my favorite bright orange life jacket commingled with all of the others during the frenzied weekend. I religiously adopted the habit of never going out alone on any of our boats without wearing that life jacket.

I lowered the boat from its lift into the lake and jumped in only to discover that the boat was quickly filling with water. I soon discovered my son-in-law, who had carefully secured the boat before going home, had removed the drain plug so that the boat would not accumulate rainwater. I jumped out quickly, raised the boat and inserted the plug.

Then I lowered the boat a second time, jumped in and started the motor. It was an eighteen-horse Mercury. Just that weekend, Paul and I had repaired its starter. The Merc was an excellent motor for that boat, but it made the boat very lively if just one person was aboard – one of the reasons for always wearing my personal life jacket.

Several inches of water were sloshing around my feet. I reached for the sponge, but then remembered Paul saying the easiest way to drain a boat is to pull the drain plug when the boat is up to speed. The boat is then at an angle where the water can flow to the back and out through the hole for the drain plug.

Knowing Paul would be waiting for me at the landing, I decided to follow his advice and drain the water while I was underway rather than taking the time to go back to the dock. So, I did just that and soon the water was mostly gone. About halfway across the lake, I reached for the plug resting on the bottom of the boat to re-install it, and what? The next thing I knew, I was airborne going over the left side of the boat into the lake and the boat was continuing on its course. In reaching for the plug, I must have unwittingly bumped the tiller handle that put the boat into a sharp turn.

When I surfaced, gasping for breath, and clearing water from my lungs, I saw the boat coming back at me! I instantly thought to myself, this is what is called the Circle of Death. Am I going to be run over and lose my life by the very boat and motor that I had given new life to just a few days before? Is this the way I am going to die, alone in the middle of the lake?

I tried to assess my position relative to the course of the boat to decide which way to swim to avoid being struck by the boat and hacked up by the propeller. I also looked around to see if there was anyone nearby who could help me. No one was in sight.

I then realized that with just a few strokes, I could position myself to the left of the boat and try to grab the side as it passed by me. That could be my ticket out of the lake. I made a desperate lunge and succeeded. Now I was cruising along at a good clip, clinging to the side of the circling boat. I decided to make my way, hand over hand, toward the stern until I could reach the stop button in the end of the tiller handle, which fortunately was facing in my direction.

To my great relief, the motor responded and stopped. Now I had a moment to just hang on, catch my breath, and relax. I took another look around to see if anyone was coming to my rescue. Still, no sign of anyone on the lake and it was getting dark.

I said to myself, "Jerry, you have to get into this boat somehow, it's your only way out of this." But, for all of my effort, I just couldn't climb high enough to get over the side of the boat. I was floating with just the top of my shoulders at the water level and the Lund S-14 has very high sides. I decided my best way back into the boat would be over the transom that is a few inches lower. I worked my way back, hand over hand again, not daring to let go of the boat for a moment because I knew I did not have the endurance to swim to shore.

I tried several times to climb over the transom, but just couldn't make it. So, I rested a bit to catch my breath again. Then, I made a lunge with all the strength I could muster and managed to catch the bottom of the life jacket on the top of the transom. I was able to teeter there but I still was not safely in the boat. I tried several times to raise myself up the rest of the way, but I couldn't manage it. Finally, I realized that this was my only way out, so I gave one more hard kick and rose up just enough to tip myself headfirst into the boat. What a relief. I was safe!

Then I realized that during that time I was trying to get back in it, the boat was filling with water and gradually sinking. The plug was still not in place and now there was about four inches of water in the boat. Where was that plug? Ah, there it was, sloshing around in the bottom. I gave another huge sigh of relief when I was finally able to put it in place. Then I just sat there pondering what I had just been through and realized my guardian angels must have been working overtime to help me.

I re-started the motor and decided to just cruise slowly the rest of the way with the water lapping at my feet. When I reached the landing, Paul was standing on the dock with the trailer waiting in the lake. He said, "What took you so long?" All I could say was, "I got thrown out of the boat!" Then he saw that I was dripping wet – my shirt, my shorts, my shoes and socks, and he said, "But you didn't lose your glasses!" Up until that moment, it hadn't even occurred to me that my glasses were still on my face.

Paul told me to just stay in the boat while he connected the trailer winch rope and he cranked me and the boat onto the trailer. Actually, at that moment, I couldn't have climbed out of the boat. I simply didn't have any physical strength left. When we got to dry land, I managed to crawl over the side, shivering at the thought of what nearly happened.

Paul, always the prepared son, gave me a towel to dry myself and to sit on while we drove back to the house. I did not look forward to telling telling Lorraine what I had just been through. Knowing her possible reaction, Paul asked if I was going to tell her. I said, "My wet clothes are going to need an explanation. Besides, I think I really need to talk about it."

After that, Paul and I went outside and analyzed what had caused the boat to behave as it did. We discovered that the steering torque adjustment was looser than it should have been.

191

There was almost no resistance to prevent the motor from turning itself. Secondly, we found the trim tab on the motor that should have kept it running a straight course was a loose and ineffective.

Apparently, I had exerted just a little turning force on the tiller when I reached for the drain plug and the turning torque of the motor did the rest, putting the boat into a sharp turn and tossing me out when I leaned over to pick up the drain plug.

I owe my life to that favorite orange life jacket. Now it is very special to me. And still to this day I give thanks to my over-worked guardian angels for seeing me through that event – and a few others!

∽𝒩∾

THE STORY OF THE HOSTA 'PRAYING HANDS'

Registered by Jerry Williams in 1996

When Lorraine and I first started planting hostas for land-scaping our new home at Lake Hubert in 1989 we had only a few varieties. One day I saw an unusual hosta in a small nursery in nearby Pequot Lakes that had been sold to a new owner the previous year. This plant, the only one of its kind in the nursery, seemed unique to me. It lacked a identifying tag so I took it to the clerk and asked her what it was. She said, "It's a hosta." I said, "I know that, but what variety is it? "She said, "I have no idea, isn't there a tag?" I said, "No, but will you sell it?" She

192

said, "Yes." I said, "Good, how much? "She said, "How about $3.95?" I said, "Good, I'll take it."

When we got home, I started looking through my copy of *The Hosta Book* by Paul Aden, but I could not identify the plant. I planted it and watched it grow for a year. I thought it was kind of interesting and gave divisions to each of our two daughters who lived in Rochester to have backups for the plant in case I "lost" mine.

After getting really hooked on hostas over the next few years, I bought a copy of George Schmid's book, *The Genus Hosta* and started searching for the plant, but again I couldn't find anything like it. I thought it might be H. *tortifrons*, but wasn't certain until a few years later when I bought a division of H. *tortifrons* at auction from Herb Benedict.

In 1994, our Minnesota Hosta Society had a meeting at Ken Anderson's nursery near Farwell, Minnesota. Knowing Ken's expertise, I potted up two divisions of my plant to take along to ask him to identify it. When we finished lunch, I put the two pots on the table, one in front of Ken and the other in front of Hideko Gowen. They both got quite excited and Hideko asked me where I got it and if I would sell it. I said, "First, tell me what it is." They both said they had never seen it before, so I told them the story of how I found it. Then they said I should name and register it. I gave each of them one of those divisions that day, trading for some hosta I didn't have.

What would be a good name? At a family gathering, our eldest daughter suggested the name 'Praying Hands' because it reminded her of Albrecht Dürer's famous painting of his brother's gnarled hands.

In 1995, I gave a division to Walt Hoover in Loyal, Wisconsin, knowing his interest in unique hostas. Walt called me that summer to ask permission to exhibit his plant at the Midwest Regional Hosta Society Convention in Davenport, Iowa, on July 12-14, 1996. He later sent me a photo showing the plant had won a blue ribbon and Best-of-Class ribbon in the Container-Grown Division III at the cut-leaf show. That convinced me to get busy with the registration process.

It took about two years to complete the AHS registration because I didn't have experience with the process and didn't realize all the photos and data I needed to collect throughout the growing season. The process was completed late in 1996.

People have asked how I thought the plant originated. The nursery where I found it did not stock anything but basic varieties of hosta at that time. At the end of the year, anything that did not sell was just left in their pots in the display area to weather over the winter and hopefully come back the following spring, weeds and all. I think possibly this plant was the result of cross-pollination of two varieties in their display. Ken Anderson and I suspect the parents were probably H. 'Fortuneii Aureomarginata' and H. 'Lancifolia', two varieties for sale at the nursery, but there is no way that I can prove that. If that is the case, the plant is a hybrid, rather than a mutation.

Following Walt Hoover's success in exhibiting the plant, we were besieged by requests for divisions. I had divided our plants so much that none of the divisions looked very robust. Lorraine said we should not give away or sell any more divisions, yet it didn't seem right to keep the plant just for ourselves.

I asked several people at the AHS convention in Indianapolis for suggestions for marketing the plant. It seemed that tissue culture would be the only way to produce enough plants in the short term to satisfy the demand. We ultimately decided to let Alan and Susan Tower take over that responsibility.

In September of 1997, I dug and bundled up ten single divisions and shipped them by USPS express mail directly to the TC lab Alan worked with. He kept me informed about the progress of the plants in the lab. In October of 1998, the first plants were delivered to Alan. They were about 2-3 inches high and bore all of the desired characteristics of the mother plant. That gave Alan and me confidence the TC specimens would be valid plants in due time, so Alan included the plants in his 1999 catalog and featured the plant on the cover.

In 2011, H. 'Praying Hands' was selected by the Horticulture Society as National Perennial Plant of the Year.

✲

RECOLLECTIONS OF SOUNDS, SIGHTS AND SENSATIONS OF THE FOUR SEASONS

Written as a class assignment for Elder Collegium, April 2012

Spring

As the black and white curtain of winter is being drawn away by the warmth of our sun, a new canvas in many shades of green slowly appears, patiently waiting to be painted by nature.

The fresh canvas will soon be dotted with yellow daffodils, tulips, forsythia, and alas, the disgusting dandelions. The plants all add brightness and excitement to the picture and awaken our latent interest in gardening.

As we wander outside in the cool fresh air, we gradually become aware of sounds that we have not heard in our winter cocoons. We watch and hear robins digging for food and gathering sticks and grass for their new homes. The distinctive sound of an oriole singing from the highest branch of the tree soliciting a would-be mate to repopulate the species is a delight. The tiny wrens are so busy making new homes for themselves, all the time singing for our enjoyment while they work.

The scent of a gentle spring rain is such a pleasant change from the bone-chilling blizzards of the winter that we soon forget our recent winter suffering and look forward to the rewards of a new Spring.

✺

HAPPINESS IS...

Written as an Elder Collegium class assignment, May 2012

Always knowing that I am a child of God.
Being greeted by my dog when I open the door.
Catching a nice mess of Bluegills with my
    grandson for supper.
Discovering a convenient vacant parking spot
    when it is raining.
Enjoying a good book, a good laugh, or a good meal.
Feeling a cool breeze on my face on a hot summer day.
Getting a thoroughly restful night's sleep.
Hearing my wife call me for dinner.
Involving and training young people to work in the
    AV room at church.
Just losing some unwanted pounds.
Knowing that I am loved.
Looking up into a bright starry sky on a summer night.
My car starting right up after a sub-zero cold spell.
No unpaid bills.
Opening a letter from a long-lost friend.
Peeking at my flower seeds and seeing them break out
    into the light.
Quickly reconciling our bank statements.
Relaxing in a warm bath after a hard day's work.
Skiing down a freshly snow-covered slope in the
    Rocky Mountains.
Taking my wife out for dinner after she just finished
    ironing my shirts.
Understanding what makes my wife happy.
Visiting the birthplaces of my Swedish grandparents.
Watching the sun slip below the ocean's horizon from
    our Maui condo.
X-rays that show no cancer.
Yellow cake with chocolate frosting.
Zeroing in on the right multiple-choice answer for a test.

FAREWELL TO FANCIE

My dear Fancie, you came into this world on April 15, 2003, as a tiny black pup. You joined Lorraine and me on a cold winter day, January 11, 2004, at Lake Hubert when your breeder, Eva Marie Mitchell, delivered you to us. Prior to that our son, Paul, visited Eva to check you out for us. He loved you right away and we did too. You missed your mother at first so for several nights you slept cuddled up right next to me for warmth.

You loved your new Lake Hubert home where you could roam the woods and go down the hill to check out the lake. At first, I had to keep your leash on a long overhead wire so you wouldn't get lost, but once you had our place memorized I took that wire down. Every morning we walked the quarter-mile long driveway together to get the newspaper. When I was working outside in the garden or on the dock you were either lying within sight of me or snuggled up in Lorraine's bed next to her.

You were really special to me after Lorraine died. You missed her too, so then you stayed closer to me all the time. I especially appreciated you during that time because our house wasn't empty with you in it.

When we moved to Northfield you had to make quite an adjustment because I needed to fasten you on a line so you wouldn't get hurt by cars in the street, but you soon figured that out and you could be loose outside until you totally lost the sight in your right eye. You memorized house plan to compensate for your increasing blindness, but you used your nose and ears very effectively to navigate. When you bumped into something, you just stepped to your right and you were usually clear.

Your routine was so dependable. Every afternoon about 4:30 you found me, usually in the office, and jammed your nose into my leg meaning it was time for our walk. That was important for both of us. At mealtime I called to you and said, "Fancie, it's time to pray." Then you would come and sit next to me at the table anticipating the prayer. You knew there would be a pill in my hand in the morning for the arthritis you got from Lyme disease when you were bitten by a deer tick when you were three years old. That was followed with a T-Bonz treat that you had to hunt for after I tossed it – even downstairs.

Because you always wanted to be near me, we had three dog beds in our house: one in the office, one in the bedroom, and a third in the sunroom where we spent our evenings.

Fancie, I already miss you because it's after 4 o'clock. I credit you for my good health because you got me out for walks twice a day. You didn't care if it was raining or snowing because you always had your fur coat on ready to go. You loved our walks and you would suck up love from anyone we met and then you gave it back to them if they petted you. You were such a great dog. Having to take you to the vet today was one of the most difficult things I ever had to do. But I felt I had no good alternative, because without knowing it you were frequently stepping in front of Florraine, barely giving her time to react. Another bad fall could be the end for her and I know you would have felt badly if she were injured again.

So, my dear Fancie, you departed this world from Northfield on a nice warm summer day, June 25, 2013. But it was a very sad day for Papa Jerry to take you to the vet and to put you to sleep painlessly. It was unfortunate that you were born with a blind left eye, and then a few years ago your right eye gradually became totally blind, a genetic defect inherited from your parents and that changed a lot of our activity. Sleep well, dear friend!

Papa Jerry

❦

THREE LOVING BIRDS

One August evening after supper my tablemate, Thomas, and I sat outside on the patio at Waverly Gardens enjoying the fresh air and cool breeze. We were the only ones out there. Suddenly three small grayish-blue birds landed on the patio deck about ten feet in front of us.

The three young birds flapped their wings as they ran toward each other and formed a cluster. They wrapped their wings around each other and started jumping up and down like little children joyous at their reunion, because they had been hatched and fledged in the tree on that patio. Then they flew away, maybe looking for their parents that had abandoned the nest after their chicks were raised. Thomas and I looked at each other. "Did you see what just happened?" I had to pray and thank God for what he had allowed us to witness.

The more I think about this event, I believe there is more to it. I think God set up one of the birds as a leader of the trio because it seems they had an advance plan to meet at their former nesting place, celebrate together, and move on to another place.

The next morning, Pastor Kyle was wrapping up his Bible study and asked if anyone wanted to say something. I told the story about this unusual event that demonstrated birds can experience and show love as Thomas and I had witnessed. One of the women said she had seen something similar and said the birds were actually fighting. I said, "No! They were using their wings to show love, not their beaks to injure." The same applies for us humans when we use our arms to embrace and not our fists to injure.

※

A COLLECTION OF MY FAVORITE QUOTATIONS, SAYINGS AND MOTTOS

Smile. God Loves You.

– source unknown

Great Spirit, grant that I may not criticize my neighbor until I have walked a mile in his moccasins. – Native American prayer

God grant me the serenity to accept the things I cannot change, the courage to change the things I can, and the wisdom to know the difference. – Reinhold Niebuhr

When through one man a little more love and goodness, a little more light and truth come into the world, then that man's life has meaning. – Alfred Delp

The best things in life aren't things.
                                            – Northport Engineering

A man needs a little madness, or he never dares to cut the rope and be free. – Zorba the Greek

Nothing will ever be attempted if all possible objections must be first overcome. – Samuel Johnson

Successful people habitually do those things that unsuccessful people habitually avoid doing. – F. Judson Snell

On the debris of our despair we build our character.
                                            – Ralph Waldo Emerson

This is the beginning of a new day. God has given me this day to use as I will. I can waste it or use it for good, but what I do is important, because I am exchanging a day of my life for it. When tomorrow comes, this day will be gone forever, leaving in its place something I have traded for it. I want it to be gain, and

not loss, good, and not evil, success and not failure, in order that
I shall not regret the price that I have paid for it.

– Dr. Heartsill Wilson

Never miss an opportunity to make someone happy even if you
have to leave them alone to do it. – F. Judson Snell

If at first you don't succeed, do it the way she told you.

– Northport Engineering

Your next raise is effective when you are.

– Northport Engineering

Can I help you or would you rather make your own mistakes?

– Source Unknown

⁓⁓

SOUND SYSTEMS I INSTALLED

Cannon Falls Elementary School, Cannon Falls

This system was an expansion of the existing one to accommodate the grade school addition.

St. Ansgar's Swedish Lutheran Church, Cannon Falls

I recall I installed this system in 1949 while I was a student
at the university. I was raised in this church, and I believe this
was the first sound system in that church. If my memory serves,
I installed Electro-Voice dynamic mics on the pulpit and the

lectern. The amplifier was a Bogen tube-type, probably 20 or 35 watts with four channels. There were no transistor amplifiers yet. The eight-inch speakers were mounted in walnut-color wooden baffles along the side walls and the cables were exposed. I cringe when I think of it now, but the congregation was satisfied with it at the time.

Vasa Lutheran Church, Vasa, Minnesota
Similar situation to St. Ansgar's Lutheran Church.

Spring Garden Lutheran Church, Near Cannon Falls
Also similar to St. Ansgar's Lutheran Church.

St. Timothy Lutheran Church, Roseville
This system was probably installed in 1952 or 1953 while we were members of this church and living in Roseville. I had help from Norm Holt, chief engineer at Telex at the time, and also a member of the congregation. I don't remember much about the system, but it was similar to the one in St. Ansgar's because that was the extent of my knowledge at that time.

Normandale Lutheran Church, Edina
The first installation was in 1958 shortly after we moved to Edina and joined the church. It was in the "first unit" building, long since torn down. I made many more installations in this church prior to moving to Lake Hubert.

Lutheran Church of the Cross, Nisswa, 1987-2007

The church had an adequate system when we joined, but the equipment was made by Executone, a telephone manufacturer, and the microphones were unique to that brand. They used 4-pin connectors instead of the standard 3-pins and required power from the system, so no standard mics were compatible with the system. The lavalier mics were very noisy when they were handled, and the speakers did not give good coverage. There was no provision to attach any other source of sound to it. The major problem was that it had been donated and installed by a current member, a crotchety old man. However, Pastor Anderson told me to proceed with any changes I thought would be helpful.

Valley Grove Lutheran Church, Northfield, 2011

❦

HOW A CHRISTIAN SHOULD MANAGE
HIS OR HER MONEY

Prepared for Normandale Lutheran Church Women
October 1980

In introducing me tonight, Ruth recited some of my background. You may think that some of those experience credentials would qualify me to talk on this subject of how a Christian should manage his or her money. They do not.

Some of you are aware I have other credentials. God has blessed Lorraine and me with an abundance that places us in the higher income tax brackets. There are even some people here who believe I actually retired from Control Data at the tender age of 51 and maybe that fact qualifies me to talk on this subject. Well, that's not really true. As a matter of fact, the pension doesn't start until I'm 65, so in the meanwhile I still have to keep on working, and I would not want it any other way. But none of those financial credentials qualify me to be here tonight either.

Instead of those, I claim only three credentials for my being able to talk to you tonight about how a Christian should manage his or her money. My first credential is that I am a Christian; that is, I am a child of God who has accepted His Son, Jesus Christ, as my Lord and Savior. Secondly, I possess a Bible, God's revealed Word to us, and thirdly, I've read all of it and am beginning to understand some of it.

The manner in which a Christian manages money has nothing to do with how much or little of it they have accumulated. The simple fact is, as Christians, we are all stewards of God's varied grace and should take direction from our Master. I'll elaborate on that point as I go on.

I must say I don't, as a rule, like to talk about, or dwell on my money and I'll tell you why. I learned through Bill Gothard's *Advanced Leadership Seminar* that my motivational gift from God is the gift of service. You know about the other gifts of the Spirit. They are described in Romans 12 and I Corinthians 12. A good servant knows whatever he has, has only been entrusted to him by his master. So, for us, whatever Lorraine and I have, we regard as belonging to God. He has been gracious enough to entrust us to manage it for him. It is not my money, nor our money, but His money.

Further, I feel that I am under heavy responsibility to Him to manage His money wisely. Recall for a minute, the parable Jesus told in Matthew 25 about the talents entrusted to the three servants. To one servant, the master gave five talents; to another servant he gave two talents; to the third servant, he gave one talent. Then the master went away on a journey. When he returned, he called the servants to see how they had handled his money. The servant to whom he gave five talents doubled it to ten, the servant who had received two talents had doubled it to four. To both of these he said well done, good and faithful servant. You have been faithful over a little, I will set you over much. Enter into the joy of the master.

Do you remember what the third servant did? He buried the one talent to protect it so it wouldn't get lost or stolen. The master chastised this servant telling him that the least he could have done would be to invest it with the bankers so he could have drawn interest upon his return. He took the talent from him and gave it to the one who had ten talents. Jesus went on to say in Matthew 25:29, *For to everyone who has, will more be given, and he will have it in abundance; but from him who has not, even what he has will be taken away.* Worse than that, the worthless servant was cast into the outer darkness – discarded as useless.

I feel very deeply that whatever we have been given is merely a trust from Him to use and develop for Him in the best way we know how. So, for me to tell you that my way of managing money is the right way is presumptuous. God will be the judge of whether or not I have served Him well, and that is why I hesitate to talk about money – it's really His role to decide if I'm doing it well.

As I was contemplating what I would say to you ladies on the subject of Christian management of money, I pondered my ongoing relationship with your husbands. In that regard I came to two conclusions. First, I decided that I would tell you what my attitude is toward the management of money based primarily on my understanding of scripture. So, don't go home and say that Jerry Williams said we should do thus and so, because I'll deny it. You can go home, though, and say Jerry believes or does thus and so.

Secondly, in order to make certain that I'm not misquoted and for those of you who want specifics, I have reproduced some practical suggestions that I will give you so that you can take them home. But, more than those, on the same handout, I have reproduced some scripture references that are the basis for my attitudes on the management of money. I'll refer to them tonight. So, you need not take notes and you will be able to go home and have the basis for a meaningful dialogue using the best textbook ever written on the subject.

Now let's get into the basis of my attitudes on the topic of money. Let's begin with several passages that put money in perspective for me. For a start, God doesn't want us to worry about whether we will have enough to live on. In the sermon on the Mount, Jesus made this very clear. Allow me to read Matthew 6:25-34.

Therefore, I tell you, do not worry about your life, what you will eat or what you will drink, or about your body, what you will wear. Is not life more than food and the body more than clothing? Look at the birds of the air; they neither sow nor reap nor gather into barns, and yet your heavenly Father feeds them. Are you not of more value than they? And can any of you by worrying add a single hour to your span of life? And why do you worry about clothing? Consider the lilies of the field, how they grow; they neither toil nor spin, yet I tell you, even Solomon in all his glory was not clothed like one of these. But if God so clothes the grass of the field, which is alive today and tomorrow is thrown into the oven, will he not much more clothe you – you of little faith? Therefore, do not worry, saying, 'What will we eat?' or 'What will we drink?' or 'What will we wear?' For it is the Gentiles who strive for all these things; and indeed your heavenly Father knows that you need all these things. But strive first for the kingdom of God and his righteousness, and all these things will be given to you as well. So do not worry about tomorrow, for tomorrow will bring worries of its own. Today's trouble is enough for today. (Also quoted in Luke 12:22-31.)

Those verses are the principal basis for my attitudes, but let's put some more props in place. Again, from the same source, we read Matthew 6:19-21: *Do not store up for yourselves treasures on earth, where moth and rust consume and where thieves break in and steal; but store up for yourselves treasures in heaven, where neither moth nor rust consumes and where thieves do not break in and steal. For where your treasure is, there your heart will be also.*

In those two passages we are told not to worry about our

earthly needs and not to put emphasis on the accumulation of wealth. Why? Jesus went on to say in Matthew 6:24, "No one can serve two masters; for a slave will either hate the one and love the other or be devoted to the one and despise the other. You cannot serve God and wealth."

So, whom shall you and I serve? I like the way Joshua said it to the children of Israel as they prepared to enter the promised land. Joshua 24:15, "Choose this day whom you will serve – but, as for me and my house, we will serve the Lord."

There are several other places in the Bible that illustrate there is a problem trying to serve both God and the things of this world. Paul was clear on this in I Timothy 6:6-10, "Of course, there is great gain in godliness combined with contentment; for we brought nothing into the world, so that we can take nothing out of it; but if we have food and clothing, we will be content with these. But those who want to be rich fall into temptation and are trapped by many senseless and harmful desires that plunge people into ruin and destruction. For the love of money is a root of all kinds of evil, and in their eagerness to be rich some have wandered away from the faith and pierced themselves with many pains."

We learn from these verses there is nothing wrong with having money as such. It is the love of money that creates the problem. Let's explore a few specific areas concerning money.

On Borrowing and Lending Money

The Bible has quite a few references that address the borrowing and lending of money. Most are in the book of Proverbs. I have found great wisdom and enjoyment in the book of Proverbs. Did you know that it has 31 chapters? That's one for each day of the month. You can read a chapter in less than ten minutes. It's a great way to read this book. It's also a good way to begin the day, because it contains such practical wisdom. To make it more interesting, read it out of one translation for the first month, then repeat it during several successive months using other translations.

Let's sample it the book of Proverbs. Proverbs 22:7 says, "The rich rule over the poor and the borrower is slave of the lender."

You see, Solomon, the acknowledged author of Proverbs recognized that borrowing demeans the spirit of the borrower. It also immediately changes the relationship between the two people. The book goes further and speaks against countersigning for another.

Proverbs 22:26-27: "Be not one of those who give pledges, who become surety for debts. If you have nothing with which to pay, why should your bed be taken from under you?"

This same concept repeats in another reference, with even more picturesque language. Proverbs 6:1-5: "My child, if you have given your pledge to your neighbor, if you have bound yourself to another, you are snared by the utterance of your lips, caught by the words of your mouth. So do this, my child, and save yourself, for you have come into your neighbor's power: go, hurry, and plead with your neighbor. Give your eyes no sleep and your eyelids no slumber; save yourself like a gazelle from the hunter, like a bird from the hand of the fowler."

Another reference is just as strong. Proverbs 11:15: "He who gives surety for a stranger will smart for it, but he who hates suretyship is secure."

I wish I had known these three passages fifteen years ago, because I can reaffirm from first-hand experience that they are absolutely true. There were two people, one a comparative stranger, the other a close relative to whom I lent money. In both cases, repayment took years to resolve, instead of the few months agreed upon. In both cases the personal relationships were badly injured. In the case of the relative, it became a source of friction within our own home, because Lorraine had advised me against making the loan.

In the other instance, I countersigned a note at a bank to keep the man from going to jail because of a bad business debt his partner had left him with. The only reason I did this was because the man showed outward signs that he had become a Christian. When the note was due and the man was nowhere to be found, you know who paid! So, my advice is don't compete with the banks and don't think that you are a better judge of a man's ability to repay than the bank.

Paul, in the book of Romans, reaffirms these views on borrowing. Romans 13:8: "Owe no one anything, except to love one another; for he who loves his neighbor has fulfilled the law." What Paul is saying is that there is a better way.

We'll go back to the book of Proverbs for the clue. Proverbs 3:27-28: "Do not withhold good from those to whom it is due, when it is in your power to do it. Do not say to your neighbor, "Go and come again, tomorrow I will give it," when you have it with you."

What Solomon is telling us is that it is better for us to make a gift instead of a loan if we have the means to do so. Then we do not have disappointed expectations. Instead, we have joy at being able to help another in distress and God will bless us for our giving.

On Taxes

What about taxes? What should the Christian's attitude be about paying taxes? Do you remember how Jesus handled that question when the Pharisees tried to ensnare him? The Pharisees were the strict legalists of the Jewish tradition. Matthew 22:16b-22:

> "Teacher, we know that you are sincere, and teach the way of God in accordance with truth and show deference to no one; for you do not regard people with partiality. Tell us, then, what you think. Is it lawful to pay taxes to the emperor, or not?" But Jesus, aware of their malice, said, "Why are you putting me to the test, you hypocrites? Show me the coin used for the tax." And they brought him a denarius. Then he said to them, "Whose head is this, and whose title?" They answered, "The emperor's." Then he said to them, "Give therefore to the emperor the things that are the emperor's, and to God the things that are God's." When they heard this, they were amazed; and they left him and went away.

While we are at this point in the Bible, I must share a thought. Right after this previous episode, the Sadducees, who were the wealthy political priests, also came to Jesus with what they thought was a complex legal and religious question. Jesus response was a classic. It was what the man who shared it with me called:

The Formula for Failure

What Jesus said to these men is written in Matthew 22:29, "You are wrong because you know neither the scripture nor the power of God." This is one verse you can take out of context and use every day. The person who does not know the scriptures or the power of God is living the Formula for Failure. Later I'll tell you the Formula for Success that is also in the Bible.

Back to the tax issue. Some people think that if they don't agree with the governing authorities, that made the tax laws, or don't think that the tax is fair that you shouldn't pay it. The Bible is also very clear on this point. Paul says it in Romans 13:1-7.

Let every person be subject to the governing authorities; for there is no authority except from God, and those authorities that exist have been instituted by God. Therefore, whoever resists authority resists what God has appointed, and those who resist will incur judgment. For rulers are not a terror to good conduct, but to bad. Do you wish to have no fear of the authority? Then do what is good, and you will receive its approval; for it is God's servant for your good. But if you do what is wrong, you should be afraid, for the authority does not bear the sword in vain! It is the servant of God to execute wrath on the wrongdoer. Therefore, one must be subject, not only because of wrath but also because of conscience. For the same reason you also pay taxes, for the authorities are

God's servants, busy with this very thing. Pay to all what is due them – taxes to whom taxes are due, revenue to whom revenue is due, respect to whom respect is due, honor to whom honor is due.

So if you have a problem with paying your taxes next April, re-read this passage. While I normally like to choose charitable organizations I support, and while most of those charitable organizations send us nice thank-you notes, I'll gladly support our government. After having made many trips to Europe and one trip to the Orient, there is no doubt in my mind that we live in the best country on earth and have the best government and politicians that money can buy.

The Special Problems of the Rich

Strange as it may seem, rich people do have problems, and it should not be surprising that the Bible speaks to some of these problems. Jesus spoke of at least one of these problems during his earthly ministry.

Mark 10:25: "It is easier for a camel to go through the eye of a needle than for a rich man to enter the kingdom of God." You might wonder why that might be the case. Jesus provided the answer in the parable of the sower. Recall that some of the seed fell among the thorns. The seed started to sprout, but soon the thorns grew up and choked the seedlings out.

Jesus explained it this way in Matthew 13:22, "As for what was sown among the thorns, this is he who hears the word, but the cares of this world and the delight in riches chokes out the word and it proves unfruitful."

That is the danger in being rich. We who have been blessed with wealth are tempted to keep one eye on our wealth instead if both eyes on the One who provided the wealth. The prophet Jeremiah knew this also. He explained it in Jeremiah 9:23, "Thus says the Lord, "Let not the wise man glory in his wisdom, let not the mighty man glory in his might, let not the rich man glory in his riches, but let him who glories, glory in this, that he understands and knows Me, that I am the Lord who practices steadfast love, justice, and righteousness in the earth, for in these things I delight," says the Lord."

If it is not enough for the rich man to have those pressures, there are other pressures. King Solomon was aware of them because he was a rich man. Proverbs 14:20: "The poor man is disliked even by his neighbor, but the rich man has many friends." Does that say something about the character of some a rich man's friends? King Solomon was also aware of the dangers of wealth, particularly wealth quickly attained.

Proverbs 11:28: "He who trusts in his riches will wither, but the righteous will flourish like a green leaf."

Proverbs 13:11: "Wealth hastily gotten will dwindle, but he who gathers little by little will increase it."

Proverbs 15:16: "Better is a little with the fear of the Lord than great treasure and trouble with it."

The Special Problems of the Poor

Tevye, the farmer in the play Fiddler on the Roof, said, "Dear God, I realize it's no shame to be poor, but it's no great honor either, so what would be so terrible if I had a small fortune?" I suppose everyone who thinks they are poor has similar thoughts at one time or another.

The Bible makes only half as many references to poor people as it does to the rich. While most of the references to the rich are warnings, most of the references to the poor are consolation, challenge, or chastisement. Let's examine them in reverse order starting with chastisement and challenge. We will learn more from them.

Proverbs 10:4-5: "A slack hand causes poverty, but the hand of the diligent makes rich. A son who gathers in summer is prudent, but a son who sleeps in harvest brings shame."

Isaiah 1:19: "If you are willing and obedient, you shall eat the good of the land."

Proverbs 28:13: "He who conceals his transgressions will not prosper, but he who confesses and forsakes them will attain mercy." That verse says to me that confession of sin is a prerequisite to prosperity. James, the brother of Jesus, in his epistle writes in James 1:7-8 said, "A double-minded man, unstable in all his ways, will not receive anything from the Lord."

James 4:2b-3: "You do not have because you do not ask. You ask and do not receive, because you ask wrongly, to spend it on your passions. Unfaithful creatures! Do you not know that friendship with the world is enmity with God?" He goes on in verses 7 to 9 to say, "Submit yourselves therefore to God. Resist the devil and he will flee from you. Draw near to God and He will draw near to you."

The book of Hebrews picks up this point in Hebrews 11:6: "Without faith it is impossible to please Him, for whoever would draw near to God must believe that He exists and that He rewards those who seek Him."

Earlier I said I would give you the Formula for Success after I had given you the Formula for Failure. It is found in Joshua 1:8. "This book of the law shall not depart out of your mouth, but you shall meditate on it day and night, that you may be careful to do according to all that is written in it; for then you shall make your way prosperous, and then you shall have good success."

What those verses say clearly to me is that if you think that you are poor and that you deserve more, then it would be good to examine your relationship to God and His Son, Jesus Christ. In a nutshell, they all say that obedience comes before blessing. Obedience to God means knowing His will and doing it.

How do we know His will? We learn it through study of the Word and prayer. So, there is the challenge. We must draw near to God. We must show him that we can be faithful over a little at first and then He promises to give us greater responsibility. Acts 17:27b-28: "Yet he is not far from each one of us, for in Him we live, and move and have our being."

By way of warning, or perhaps consolation, the Bible cautions against striving for wealth for the sake of wealth. Proverbs 23:4-5: "Do not toil to acquire wealth, be wise enough to desist. When your eyes light upon it, it is gone; for suddenly it takes to itself wings, flying like an eagle toward heaven."

Recall also the warning to the rich for it is also of consolation to the poor. Proverbs 15:16: "Better is a little with the fear of the Lord, than great treasure and trouble with it."

On Contributions

The early Mosaic books of the Bible are very clear on the responsibility of God's people to return a portion of their blessings to God. The 27th chapter of Leviticus and the 14th chapter of Deuteronomy set forth in specific detail how ten percent of the seed, fruit, animals and land are to be returned to God each year. That is the tithe of the Old Testament.

Very early in our marriage, Lorraine and I were blessed with a pastor who challenged us to try proportionate giving, using the tithe as our goal. We not only took Pastor Anderson's challenge seriously, we also took the promise of scripture seriously. I can tell you from first-hand experience that God delivers on his promises. I'd like to share the verses with you that Pastor Anderson shared with us. But before I do that, I must tell you that we didn't have the courage or faith to start immediately with ten percent. At that time our giving level was only two percent. I recall that we started with five percent that first year. The next year we raised it to six percent, and so on until we reached the tithe. Now here those verses that Pastor Anderson shared with us from

Malachai 3:10: "Bring the full tithe into the storehouse, so that there may be food in my house, and thus put me to the test, says the Lord of hosts; see if I will not open the windows of heaven for you and pour down for you an overflowing blessing. I will rebuke the locust for you, so that it will not destroy the produce of your soil; and your vine in the field shall not be barren, says the LORD of hosts."

Jesus reaffirmed this promise in Luke 6:28: "Give and it will be given to you, good measure, pressed down, shaken together, running over, will be put into your lap. For the measure you give will be the measure you get back."

King Solomon understood this. In the book of Proverbs he wrote about it several times. Proverbs 3:9-10: "Honor the Lord with your substance and with the first fruits of all your produce; then your barns will be filled with plenty and your vats bursting with wine."

You will have to make the translation from an agrarian society to our modern money-based economy. The Proverbs are structured in a unique way, usually giving both sides of the issue as illustrated in this next verse. Proverbs 11:24: "One man gives freely yet grows all the richer; another withholds what he should give, and only suffers want."

Another example of this two-edged prose is in Proverbs 28:27: "He who gives to the poor will not want, but he who hides his eyes will get many a curse."

Think of that verse in connection with America's willingness to give refuge to the Vietnamese, Laotians, Cubans and Haitians. Think of it also in connection with those in need in your community and your neighborhood.

One year, as Lorraine and I contemplated where some of our extra giving might go, she said, "What about Judy?" I responded, "Judy who?" She said, "Our niece." I had gotten so accustomed to focusing on tax-deductible charities, that I wasn't even conditioned to think of gifts to individuals within the family. This young lady, who was trying to raise and support a two-year old son by herself was desperately in need of help to meet dental and medical expenses. The amount we sent to her turned out to be very nearly the amount she was short, even though we didn't know it at the time. I'm sure the Lord did though. We also learned later that she had been praying that somehow this financial burden would be lifted. Can you imagine what that gift did for her faith? And the thrill it gave us? And the IRS didn't even know about it because it wasn't tax-deductible.

Some Practical Suggestions

Now that we have laid a firm foundation with scripture as our footing, I'll give you dozen thoughts that are part of my mode of practical money management. Some you may agree with, some you may disagree with, but as I said at the beginning, these are the convictions Lorraine and I agree upon.

1. Don't spend it. That is, until you ask yourself, would I buy this if Jesus were standing at my side because, believe it or not, He truly is there. That doesn't mean we have to pinch-pennies; it just puts the potential purchase in Christian perspective so that you won't have guilt feelings later.

2. Take time to think – at least about major purchases. Some purchases come with strings attached, like maintenance costs, or decorating consistency, or space rearrangement. I remember when we decided to get a larger bed. It ultimately meant replacing all the bedroom furniture, carpeting the floor and repainting the whole room!

3. Buy good value. In my book, it's just poor stewardship to buy something cheap that you'll be dissatisfied with and ulti-

mately have to replace. We have never been sorry for the good furniture and appliances we bought.

4. Ask for help. Our son, Paul, says he learned that experience is the best teacher because it's the most expensive. Benefit from someone else's expensive experience and save your money.

5. Plan your purchases together, if you are a family. Two heads are better than one. This will avoid mistakes and it makes getting the item more exciting and rewarding when you finally have it. Some of you have noticed and commented on our new driveway. Well, it's the result of planning, taking our time, asking for help, and buying good value. We needed to replace the driveway at least two years ago. Fortunately, our friends were polite enough not to point it out. The problem was that Lorraine wanted blacktop and I wanted concrete. At least, that's what I thought.

Because we couldn't agree, we didn't do anything. After two years, I got a bright idea and said, "Would you accept concrete if I put blacktop sealer over it?" She said yes. What I discovered was that she didn't really care what it was, she just wanted a black driveway because it would look better with our house. Once I understood that I had an even better idea. Having sat on the church's committee to explore improving the parking lot landscape, I had learned about the Bowmanite process with colored concrete made to look like black cobblestone. So, we got the wise counsel of my brother-in-law who is an architect. He pointed us to the man who handled the product. From there it was just a matter of patiently waiting for a year and half for his schedule.

222

6. Resist impulse buying. Don't let merchandisers manipulate your mind. Make a shopping list and stick to it unless you see something that you forgot to put on the list. Well-decorated and arranged stores today are fun to shop in, but they can make a shambles of your budget if you don't use self-control. Just don't carry it to extremes so you can't have a little fun now and then.

7. There's nothing wrong with used merchandise if you know what you are buying. Three of our last four cars were used when we bought them, but because I knew that particular make inside and out, I had no apprehension and they were good buys for us at the time.

8. Don't throw it away, if it can be fixed or passed on to someone else who needs it. The old saying "waste not, want not" fits here. The only danger lies in a law that I have observed. That is, stuff will accumulate to the extent there is no room to store it. Our attic is full of deferred decisions – but many times I have found just the part I needed to keep something else going.

9. Do it yourself. Don't hire things done that you can do for yourself. Home projects provide opportunity for learning and satisfaction. They also provide opportunities for teaching your children how to work with their hands. A secondary benefit is that it provides the opportunity for meaningful time together, something your children will long remember. My philosophy is that if I can get a book on the subject or find someone who can teach me, I can learn. But again, this can be carried to extremes and the rule may fail. Time is money, both to you and those you hire. You need to make the judgment where it applies.

10. Don't pay interest or finance charges, except on a home

mortgage or an emergency automobile purchase. This also means, don't buy on the installment plan. Don't, under any circumstances, live beyond your income level! Instead, save your money until you can pay cash. You'll get more satisfaction when you can buy the item with your saved money and you can often get a better deal with cash.

11. Be careful about insurance. There is a place for insurance – just buy only the protection you need. Trust the Lord to protect you and your possessions. If you turn them over to Him, He will watch over His own.

12. Make your money work for you. Don't let your money sit idle. Find good investments. This takes work and study. Bill Gothard helped me in this regard concerning the stock market. I have made a lot of money in the stock market, and I have lost a lot of money in the stock market. On balance, I'm ahead, but the stocks I made the most money on were the stocks of the companies where I was employed, and I didn't just take a flying gamble. What Bill said made good sense to me: "In the stock market, God has to bless too many other people to get to you." That may make my stockbroker friends unhappy, but I have come to believe it.

Conclusion

There you have it. As I said at the outset, I was reluctant to agree to the request to speak on this topic, but I realized I could use the opportunity to share my beliefs on money management based on scripture and let the Bible speak instead. I hope it may have been helpful or, at least, will stimulate you to think about your money management in a new light.

Chapter 14

MY FAMILY

My Grandparents

Alvin (originally Albin) Williams (originally Peterson) was born February 22, 1868, at Alviken farm in Gränna parish, Jönköping, Sweden. Because his father was named Carl Johan Petersson, Albin's patronymic name in Sweden would have been Carlsson, but when the family came to the United States in 1869, they were all called Peterson. Because there were so many of that name where they lived in Pierce County, Wisconsin, Alvin and two of his brothers changed their surname to Williams, anglicized from Wilhelm, the oldest brother's middle name.

On January 23, 1895, Albin married Hulda Susanna Larson (originally Larsdotter) of St. Paul at Svea Lutheran Church in Pierce County. Hulda was born December 30, 1870, at Näbben farm, Hova parish, Skaraborg, Sweden. She immigrated in 1889. Alvin and Hulda had four children: Lawrence "Stanley,"

Alvin and Hulda Williams

Marland, Olga, and Jewell. While the family lived in Wisconsin,

Alvin farmed and later ran the Alvin Williams General Merchandise store that sat kitty-corner from the Svea Church. When they moved to St. Paul in 1918, he ran a grocery store and later worked in shipping for a toy manufacturer. Alvin died on June 15, 1936, and Hulda passed on July 27, 1945. They are buried in Union Cemetery in Maplewood, Minnesota.

John (originally Johan) Henning Strom (originally Ström) was born December 23, 1867, at Västerhäljatorp farm in Hova parish, Skaraborg, Sweden. He immigrated in 1888. On September 1, 1894, he married Mathilda "Tillie" Johnson (originally Jonsdotter) in St. Paul. She was born September 21, 1871, at Hådala farm in Västra Torsås parish, Kronoberg, Sweden, and immigrated in 1889. John and Tillie had six children: Alfer, Herman, Elmie, Ralph, Evelyn, and a baby boy who did not survive. John worked most of his life as a driver for the St. Paul Fire Department. He died April 12, 1952, in

John and Tillie Strom

St. Paul. Tillie died on March 5, 1965, in Inver Grove. They are also buried in Union Cemetery.

My Parents

Marland Reinhold Williams, M.D., was born June 5, 1899,

on the family farm in Trenton Township, Pierce County, Wisconsin. On August 11, 1923, he married Elmie Mildred Strom who was born January 21, 1899, in St. Paul. They had three children together: me, Keith, and Marilyn. For 45 years, Marland served the community of Cannon Falls, Minnesota, as the town physician. He died August 22, 1994, in Eustis, Lake County, Florida, and was laid to rest in the Cannon Falls Community Cemetery. Elmie was born January 21, 1899, in St. Paul. Elmie died June 20, 1934, in St. Paul and is buried in Union Cemetery.

On July 14, 1936, Marland married my stepmother, Viola Elizabeth Grisim, who was born September 10, 1906 in Randolph, Minnesota. Viola and Marland had a son, Roger. She died September 11, 1949, in Cannon Falls, and is buried in Union Cemetery.

Marland was married a third time on March 14, 1953, to Phyllis Esther (Wallace) Rogers, who was born May 30, 1920, in Northfield, Minnesota. Phyllis had two sons from a previous marriage, Richard Wallace and Gregory Paul. After Marland died, Phyllis moved to Arizona, where she passed away on November 30, 2002. Her ashes are buried beside Marland in Cannon Falls.

Marland and Phyllis Williams

Olga, Jewell, and Stanley Williams, also known as O.J.S., were my dad's siblings. None of them ever married, so they lived together their entire lives. In many ways, they were the glue that held the Williams clan together. "Olga-Jewell," as the youngest members of the family called them (because they were never sure which one was which) were masters at entertaining the whole family in their small house at 855 Sherwood Avenue in St. Paul. Around Christmas time, we gathered there for what we called "duppa" (dopp i gryta or dip-in-the-pot), a traditional Swedish Christmas Eve meal. The afternoon began with a cup of warm glögg (something like mulled wine) – but not too much. Duppa is boiled pork, beef, and potato sausage. Olga or Jewell would stand at the stove to ladle the resulting broth over a half-slice of Wonder Bread. This "wiener water soup," as Ken Nordaune called it, was accompanied by lingonberries, sylta, rice pudding, Jello salad, lefse, and fruit breads. The beverage was always root beer poured by Stanley. Dessert was fruit soup, fruit cake, and at least seven kinds of Christmas cookies with egg coffee brewed in a large white enamel pot on the stove. Games

Olga, Jewell and Stanley Williams

in their basement recreation room followed, with enough prizes that no one went home empty handed.

228

My Siblings

Keith Marland Williams was born April 30, 1929, in St. Paul. On September 1, 1950, he married Pauline Ardis Langvand (born January 8, 1931) in Minneapolis. Pauline died on May 7, 2007, in Grand Junction, Colorado. Keith and Pauline had two children

Keith and Pauline (Langvand) Williams

and adopted two more. Judith Ann was born August 24, 1951. Jeffrey Lawrence was born December 10, 1953. He died in an automobile accident in Florida on January 3, 1992. Deborah Louise was born July 17, 1961, and Jennifer Lynn was born March 23, 1964. Keith lives in Grand Junction, Colorado.

Marilyn Elmie (Williams) Nordaune was born October 19, 1933, in St. Paul. She married Kenneth Marvin Nordaune (born April 6, 1930) on November 5, 1955, at St. Timothy Lutheran Church in St. Paul. Ken

Marilyn (Williams) and Ken Nordaune

passed away on May 24, 2013, in Lakeville, Minnesota. Marilyn and Ken had three daughters: Vicki Marie, born February 6, 1956, Kimberly Jo, born February 11, 1959, and Dana Lynn, born October 10, 1964. Marilyn lives in Burnsville, Minnesota.

Roger "Butch" Stanley Williams was born November 26, 1937. On June 20, 1964, he married Karla Ann McGraw in St. Anthony Village. They have two daughters, Allyson Lea, born April 6, 1965, and Lindsey Nicole, born August 9, 1970. Roger and Karla divorced in 1995. On November 22, 1997, Roger married Pamela Ann Carroll in New Brighton. They later divorced. Roger lives in Shoreview, Minnesota.

Roger Williams

My Wives

Lorraine Laura (Hoffman) Williams, born December 29, 1926, in St. James, Minnesota. She married me on June 11, 1950, in St. James. She passed away on May 12, 2006, at our home on Lake Hubert. Her ashes are interred in the columbarium at Lutheran Church of the Cross in Nisswa.

Florraine Flora (Hoffman) (Wangen) (Trygstad) WILLIAMS was born December 29, 1926, in St. James. She married Joseph David Wangen (born January 6, 1924) in a double wedding with her twin sister, Lorraine, on June 11, 1950. Joe died from a heart attack on November 24, 1958, while studying in Oslo, Norway on a scholarship. Florraine and Joe had one child, Jody Rene, born February 21, 1956. Jody later became my stepdaughter and is married to Larry Joseph Hoffman. They have two children: Hillary Marta and Matthew Christian.

On June 17, 1961, Florraine married William Marcus Trygstad, D.D.S. (born December 19, 1917). His first wife, Nina

Lorraine and Florraine

Stahn, died from cancer in 1957. Bill brought two children to his marriage with Florraine: Kirsti Mae and William Marcus ("Tryg"). Kirsti has a son, Grant Marcus Trygstad, and lives in Sparta, Wisconsin. Marcus and his wife Robin Denise (nee Temple) have two children: Kristina Joy and Alexander William. They live in Spring, Texas. Bill died on January 12, 2009, and is buried in Sunset Memorial Park in St. Anthony, Minnesota.

Florraine married me on June 6, 2009, at Bethel Lutheran Church in Northfield. She passed away on November 17, 2018, and is buried beside her first husband, Joe, in Mount Hope Cemetery in St. James.

**My Children, Their Spouses, and
My Grandchildren and Great-Grandchildren**

Elizabeth Ann Williams (Wall) Gomoll, born April 19, 1952, in Red Wing, Minnesota, married Roger Dennis Gomoll (born

231

June 20, 1953) on June 3, 2006, in an airplane hangar at Anoka County Airport in Blaine, Minnesota. Liz's first husband was David Whitney Wall, M.D., born January 29, 1953. They were married on June 14, 1975, at Normandale Lutheran Church in Edina and divorced in 2001. Elizabeth and David have three children:

Elizabeth and Roger Gomoll

Svea Christine (Wall) (Kvernen) Merry, born September 7, 1977, in St. Paul, married Jonathan Hans Kvernen, M.D. (born

The Merry family (left to right): Matthew, Katie, Benjamin, Jonathan, Steve, Svea, Drew, Marielle, Katianna

July 31, 1974), on July 23, 1999, in Rochester, Minnesota. Svea and Jon had two sons, both born in La Crosse, Wisconsin: Benjamin Gerald on July 20, 2001, and Andrew Jonathan on February 15, 2004. Jon died from lung cancer in Rochester on May 1, 2004. He is buried in Oakwood East Cemetery in Rochester. On September 30, 2006, Svea married Stephen Paul Merry, M.D. (born February 14, 1961). Steve's first wife, Kayleen Elizabeth (nee Slater, born August 17, 1961), succumbed to cancer on March 9, 2006, in Rochester. He and Kayleen had five children together. Twins, Matthew Stephen and Marielle Elizabeth were born on June 24, 1993. (Matthew married Katie Anderson in 2019.) They adopted two children from Kazakhstan in 2001: Katianna Linnea, born November 10, 2000, and Karston David, born October 14, 2000. (Karston was later adopted by the Ausborn family in Iowa.) Their son Benjamin James was born March 16, 2002. After Svea and Steve were married they legally adopted each other's children. To avoid confusion with two Benjamins of similar age in the family, Benjamin Kvernen was renamed Jonathan Ben Merry. The Merry family lives in Rochester.

Matt, Sarah, Eden, Jack and Hazel Beckman

Sarah Elizabeth (Wall) Beckman, born June 16, 1980, in St. Paul, married Matthew Donald Beckman, Ph.D. (born February

12, 1984) on June 27, 2008, at Christ Presbyterian Church in Edina, Minnesota. They have three children: Eden Signe, born December 13, 2011, Jon "Jack" Matthew, born March 21, 2015, and Hazel Sarah, born August 22, 2018. The Beckmans live in State College, Pennsylvania.

Peter James Wall, born April 18, 1983, in Chicago, Illinois, married Elizabeth "Betsy" Ann Petersen (born May 2, 1983) on September 17, 2005, in North Saint

Pete, Betsy, Grace and Zach Wall

Paul. They have two children, Grace Marjorie, born January 9, 2013, and Zachary Peter, born August 17, 2016. The Wall family lives in Rochester.

Susan Carol (Williams) Jenkins, M.D., was born June 12,

Jenkins Family, L-R: Chris, Sam, Kat, Sue and Bob

1955, in Red Wing, Minnesota. On June 24, 1979, she married Robert Brian Jenkins, M.D., Ph.D. (born October 23, 1955) at Normandale Lutheran Church in Edina. They live in Rochester. They have two children, Christopher Lawrence, born December 9, 1982, and Katherine "Kat" Rae, born May 9, 1987, and married to Samuel James Lauer on May 20, 2017, in Rochester. Chris, Kat and Sam live in the Twin Cities.

Paul Marland Williams was born October 21, 1957, in Northfield, Minnesota. On June 26, 1993, he married Evone Kelmia Greene (born February 28, 1952) in the living room of our home on Lake Hubert. They live in Independence, Minnesota.

Paul and Evone (Greene) Williams

EPILOGUE
by Jerry's daughter Susan
June 12, 2020

This book was largely a team effort by Dad and Liz; I was lucky to help with proof-reading. I already knew these stories, but I feel closer to Dad for having revisited them through his eyes.

Dad has always been an upbeat, happy man. Despite having lost his mother in childhood, he grew up with a feeling of being blessed and cared for. He loved the Lord, married well, and worked hard to develop his skills and knowledge in whatever task he chose to pursue. There were challenges to be faced – it is typical of him to discount those in this narrative.

Dad did not mention the many people whom he mentored over his lifetime. This began in the computer and technical industries, continued through Williams Sound, and in his later years he was delighted to be able to mentor high school students in running the audio-visual system at Bethel Lutheran Church. They, along with us as his privileged children, are his legacy. Since moving to the Parkview West in the Northfield Retirement Community, it has become clear Dad is struggling with dementia. His joyful energy has endeared him to the staff. He has again found a sound system in need of rehabilitation. And he has portraits of his beloved Lorraine and Florraine to remind him of the welcome awaiting him in heaven.

THINGS I LEARNED FROM DAD
by his son Paul
September 14, 2020

I learned many things from Dad. Some were common
things: how to ride a bike, how to cast a fishing rod, how to ski
when I was young – not much more than waist high. Back then
you got up the ski hill by a "rope tow," a thick rope that ran from
the bottom of the hill to the top, moving non-stop at a fast pace.
You stepped into the tracks left by others' skis, picked up the
rope, letting it whiz thru your mittens, then grabbed hold and
away you went. Every time I grabbed the heavy moving rope
I fell. Dad said to grab the rope gradually, but I only did face
plants. Dad still recalls that later that day I asked what "gradually" meant. We both learned something, I think.

Dad never missed a chance to teach me. Being Dad's little
guy, I always followed him around when he did things at home.
Dad made my small hands an asset. I could reach into places
that were hard for him to get to. I learned to help pull new
wires in the house, start nuts on screws, hold a light. As I grew
a bit, I watched him fix things and I wanted to do things in the
workshop. I started by cutting parts out of old radios (and a few
things I wasn't supposed to take apart). Later Dad provided lessons on soldering, stripping wires, using meters, and understanding circuits. Heathkit electronics were provided for me to build.
Dad helped me design and build some of my own ideas, too.
Many lessons on Ohm's law and engineering were provided on
the chalk board in his workshop. I have that chalkboard today.

When I wanted a radio control airplane, Dad "arranged a loan" for me and got me together with a friend of his to buy an old one I could afford. From this I learned at an early age about finance, interest, and earning money.

In his workshop I learned how to use all kinds of tools, and how to plan a project, and solve problems in making things. It wasn't until I was in college that I realized other guys my age didn't have the skills Dad had given me: how to think things through, set goals, and make a plan. Dad also taught me to look for opportunities to innovate. He provided resources to support my endeavors and advice when I asked.

Dad and I think and talk together about the world in engineering ways. Mom often complained when we got together that it was time to stop talking shop. Dad gave me so many things that have been helpful throughout my life. Those lessons and his support were what enabled me to start and run my own business. Now in my retirement, it is a real blessing to have time to have a new relationship with him. Being friends with Dad and, of course, still talking in our own language is pretty special.

※

JERRY IS A GENEROUS MAN
by his daughter Elizabeth
September 1, 2020

Two things Dad said when I was a kid have stuck with me: "Where there's a Williams there's a way," and, "Perfect is close enough." Those are tough mottos to live up to, but that is how Jerry Williams navigates life. He has (almost) always found a way to solve a problem, and he has always held himself to the highest standards. That reminds me of another of his sayings: "If it's worth doing, it's worth doing it right."

Dad is one of the most generous people I know. He is quick to help someone in financial need, tithing to his church is a given, and he is genuinely pleased to be generous to causes dear to his heart. I have benefited from his generosity many times and strive to pay it forward.

Jerry is also generous with his time. Of the five "love languages," (words of affirmation, acts of service, giving gifts, quality time, and physical touch), his language is, without a doubt, service. If something needed fixing, Dad stopped by the hardware store on his way home from work to pick up the needed part. More often than not, the broken thing was fully functional again the next day. For years, he was a devoted caretaker for both of his wives. And show him a church with a sub-par sound system, and he will make it better – much better.

I'm not sure whether Dad is more of a people person or a project person. He thrives on relationships, whether new or lifelong, which has made the social isolation brought on by the corona virus intolerable for him. He also thrives on projects and keenly feels the absence of his workshops (yes, plural workshops: wood, electrical, and mechanical). Now in full retirement mode at Waverly Gardens, he is inventing projects to keep his mind and hands busy.

Jerry Williams is a tremendous blessing to me, our family, his friends, and the community. The world is better for having him in it.

✣

Last Words

I wrote this book with the hope that by telling you how I succeeded in life, you might also do well beyond your expectations. If you make God's only son, Jesus Christ, the center of your faith life, and make it a point to become an active member of a Christian congregation and put it at the center of your social life, you will reap blessings for you and your family beyond your fondest dreams. But, remember to thank the Lord for all He has done and will do for you.

— Jerry

The Extended Williams Family, July 4, 2017

Front L–R: Grace Wall, (Kaia the dog), Drew Merry, Roger Williams, Florraine & Jerry Williams, Marilyn Nordaune
Back L–R: Betsy, Pete, Zach Wall; Matt, Ben, Katianna, Marielle, Jonathan, Steve & Svea Merry; Liz & Roger Gomoll; Evone
Greene & Paul Williams; Sue & Bob Jenkins, Kat & Sam Lauer, Chris Jenkins
Not in this picture: Matt, Sarah, Eden, Jack (and the future Hazel) Beckman; Katie, the future Mrs. Matt Merry

CREDITS

Thank you to my brother, Roger S. Williams, for the beautiful sunset photograph used on the front cover.

Thank you to St. Olaf College for permission to use "Led by the Spirit of Truth" as my book title. It is a line from the college hymn, "Fram! Fram! Kristmenn, Krossmenn."

Appreciation goes to my St. Olaf College physics lab professor, Dr. Erick Hetle, who emphasized to the young fellows in his class that they did not deserve to be called men unless they carried a pocket knife.

I have deep respect for my St. Olaf College English professor, Hjalmer Lockensgaard, who coerced me to write an essay. Here it is, a little late and for no credit!

My appreciation goes to Dr. Harold Dittmanson, my St. Olaf College religion professor who explained to me why it was all right to date an Episcopalian girl. (It didn't happen.)

Great gratitude goes to Mr. Milford J. C. Jensen, manager of St. Olaf College radio station, WCAL. He urged me to take the FCC exam for a first-class radiotelephone engineer's license so I could operate the 5,000-watt WCAL transmitter on weekends.

Special thanks to my daughters, Elizabeth and Susan, who spent many hours refining and proofreading this manuscript. Liz dedicated so much time collecting the photographs and placing them within the text. This book would not have been possible without their help and encouragement.

I very much appreciate Brent Kivell, who did a marvelous job of laying out the text and images contained in this book. His patience was boundless.

My love and thanks to my adult children and their spouses, Liz and Roger, Sue and Bob, Paul and Evone, and my sister, Marilyn Nordaune, who are showing so much love for me in my last days on earth, as I await my trip to the home that Jesus is preparing for me to join my two wonderful wives and all of my beloved family members who have preceded me.